BITS OF WISDOM

Lightworker's Log

SAM

Dedicated to seekers of the I AM Presence; the only Truth in this game of life.

CONTENTS

PREFACE

We experience and become what we persistently imagine. A better life is hard to achieve if we think the same old way. Opening the mind and thinking differently helps us to create greater possibilities. *Bits Of Wisdom* offers new ways of thinking and being. It includes edited versions of copy from the Lightworker's Log Book Series along with additional articles to nurture open minds.

ARTICLES

A Lightworker's Life

Certain traits help one to identify lightworkers. Lightworkers offer loving energy during potentially harmful situations. They no longer add energy to negative events by thinking about them but realize the focus of their awareness becomes reality. These individuals may have fewer friends of like-mind. Yet, being with friends is like heaven for everyone thinks, and focuses, on the same things making the creation of those things much faster.

Lightworkers disregard knee-jerk reactions of the past. They still their mind to connect with their True Self before considering whether to respond to what seems to be happening. They help others to realize the divinity within themselves and all living things. Seasoned lightworkers do not regularly attend events such as workshops or classes but sporadically go to add their higher frequency of light. They lead though example and may have their own events. Many congregate regularly to merge positive waves of love, wholeness, and prosperity into the earth and its inhabitants.

Life as a lightworker is much different from the usual way of living. Some seasoned lightworkers let go of relationships, jobs, homes, possessions, and other things that do not support higher states of awareness. As a result, they take back their God-given power to support new and much healthier ways of BEing. Adjusting to this kind of life is not easy. But living this way helps to stay in tune with True Self and supports a higher level of consciousness much better than a life of limitation. Honing intuitive capabilities instead of seeking help outside the True Self is common for seasoned lightworkers. Messages from *All That Is* come increasingly from within as these lightworkers find their way back to the divinity and wholeness of I AM. Life fills increasingly with peace, joy, love, harmony, and prosperity. Realize that this state of awareness is possible for everyone.

Humanity is here to experience, express, and expand the richness of *All That Is*. Lightworkers know their state of BEing is merely an increased awareness of everyone's true and natural self. All of humanity shall soon be intuitively led to seek nothing but the True Self so begin now to nourish it every chance you get.

A Nurturing Atmosphere

Atmosphere plays a major role in life no matter where we live. Remember, human bodies are 70-90% water that takes on surrounding energies. When we live in a nurturing atmosphere, it's much easier to receive guidance from our True Self, an aspect of *All That Is*. Little changes in living conditions can make a huge difference in our state of mind and overall health. Here are a few tips that make living conditions more favorable to connecting with *All That Is*.

Plants not only look appealing but also add oxygen to the air. Consider growing colorful plants and herbs indoors and a vegetable garden outside. Philodendron and other types of ivy grow well inside. African violets are another option if you remember to water them a little bit every other day. Cactus grows well without water for weeks.

Nurturing music spreads throughout the air, filling it with loving energy. Listen to several types of music to decide which type is best for you. Choose inspiring music that fills you with joy, with peace and love. Classical music, without words, helps to keep us out of the past and can be very peaceful. Spiritual and New Age music can be calming as well and fills us with joy and love.

Clutter tends to draw lower energies. We free our mind of the past, making it easier to live in the present moment, when we rid ourselves of possessions that carry strong memories. **A clean atmosphere** is much more conductive to connecting with our True Self. Colors can make a difference as well. Pastels, blue, green and yellow create calming, healing, nurturing atmospheres.

Be aware that everything has a vibration. That **vibration affects your physical body**. Scan the area where you live to identify vibrations that may be affecting you. If you notice negative changes in your mood, look around to find the cause. Do you have a lot of electronics, such as televisions, cable, or converter boxes? Unplug them and move them away from you for a month to see if it makes a difference in your state of mind.

These are but a few helpful things to improve your overall state of health and ability to communicate with what many people refer to as God or Spirit. I trust you will find them useful.

Affirmations

Thoughts manifest into things. Affirmations are positive statements to help us recognize the wholeness of which we are. Here are a few affirmations to repeat if you wish.

"The world is always offering richness and abundance, prosperity and wholeness, and I partake of it joyfully, always relishing in the knowledge that we are One."

"The richness of the earth supports us in our efforts to become One with it once again."

"I am grateful to be perfect, whole, and free, ever rejoicing in my Oneness with the Creator."

"All is well as I partake of the richness of God's bounty."

"I am one with *All That Is*, perfect, whole and free."

"I clearly see the beauty all around me and am joyful for its abundance."

"Prosperous, healthy and whole, I rejoice in the Oneness of *All*."

"I am grateful to be one with the Supreme Personality of the universe."

"All is well as I relish in the Love of the One."

"I AM the *All That Is*, perfect, whole and free."

All About Love

Many mystics note love is the force that brings the greatest positive effect. The power of love surrounds us in many ways and we need only open ourselves to its many possibilities to experience them. According to Emmanuel, the soul's greatest need is self-love, which leads us to grow and dispels judgments. Self-love helps to unify for we are unable to accept others until we accept ourselves. Loving oneself is vital so that we may learn to love others unconditionally. Upon achieving unconditional love and awareness of self, we then know how to love others.

Expansion comes through the heart. Every bit of kindness and love given to others adds more Light and power to God's Truth. We are all Good, we are all Light, and most importantly, we are all Divine Love, a part of our Creator. Having negative thoughts and acting out the separation ruse is really a call for help as one looks for love. People who act negatively offer us the opportunity to bless and unconditionally love them.

We identify mis-thought by the way we feel. If our mood is depressed, anxious, or anything but wholly joyous, we react with a lack of love allowing ego to rule. We either judge as an expression of fear, seeing the physical, or forgive, as an expression of love, recognizing our divinity. We become one with *All That Is* and our true nature by recognizing mis-thought and deciding to think otherwise. Ego's rule is over when our collective consciousness unites.

Love is the key to eternal life. We can help each other by realizing the true nature of our being, Divine Love. It is a gift, which we must give because the consciousness of love seeks a place to express itself. When Divine Love flows through us our need for others to love us diminishes. Divine Love is a state of BEing, willingness to merge and connect without force. It's a state of wholeness that reflects within, allowing us to commune outside of time and space. Eternal life is ours when we end separation, to unify in the oneness of unconditional love, as an integrated soul dedicated to total acceptance of *All That Is*.

Anchoring Energy

New energies continue to bombard us here on earth. Many of us anchor that energy just by being where we are. We always, even unknowingly, transmute denser energies into the higher vibration of Love by our presence. Several years of anchoring this energy into earth's grid taught me that it does make a difference.

Very intense frequencies permeate the planet this year during all types of earth changes, increased geomagnetic activity, planetary alignments, solar and lunar eclipses. Each event changes energies around us and needs grounding to cement the new Mother Earth. Our bodies change right along with Gaia to remain on the same wavelength.

For many years, these events worried me until physical manifestation of changed consciousness happened right before my eyes during a tornado. This occurred after several years of work to change the way I thought. Knowing that thoughts physically manifest to create the world in which we live helped me to mold a peaceful existence despite surrounding physical circumstances.

A sudden gust of strong wind prompted me to stop writing and rise from the big, brown, Lazy Boy chair to investigate one sunny 2011 day in late spring. Sounds of debris hitting solid objects resounded through the air as I walked toward the back porch. They reminded me of hurricane sounds but it was not that season so I remained unafraid.

Peace filled me even when I opened the back screen door to investigate. There, before my eyes to the right, sat a funnel cloud. Instead of cowering in fear with recognition my attention drew to a variety of objects that seemingly floated in mid-air. Pieces of wood, roof tiles, stones and other small objects swirled in the funnel as I watched in wonder. It didn't occur to me that I stood a mere twenty-feet away from a tornado as I stood with gaping mouth watching the scene.

It was so awesome that all I wanted to do was record the event so, of course, I closed my mouth and ran back into the house to get a camcorder. The funnel moved past my rented home and down the canal by the time I returned. Tiles ripped off several houses a mile away as I watched trying to video the scene in vain. And very soon, the funnel disappeared.

I reentered the house to finish the day's work but rose again hungry two hours later. Several people had strolled past the house, which was very unusual for the very quiet neighborhood. More people stood near the drive as I backed out for a quick drive to buy fresh vegetables.

Police tape and a scene from the movies sat around the corner five houses away. Maneuvering around a crowd of gaping neighbors, I headed around the tape. A quick glance to my left revealed several damaged roofs, scattered debris and ripped up lawns. The scene played out throughout the neighborhood as I made my way, sometimes driving on people's lawns, to get to the store (Yes, fresh salad is now a must!).

The telephone rang insistently as I entered the house upon returning home. "Are you alright?" my sister inquired, quickly explaining that my neighborhood, and two others, was now featured on national news for the freak tornado that ran amuck came out of nowhere.

All I could do was shake my head in wonder as I laughingly explained how the funnel cloud entertained me for several minutes. My sister could not comprehend the state of consciousness that kept me safe. No, I was crazy for not cowering in the closet upon seeing the funnel.

This illustrates a very important point for those holding the Light and anchoring new energies. We are safe in the bosom of Mother Earth despite the consciousness of others seemingly apart from us. It makes no difference where we live for when we hold the Light with true Oneness consciousness no threat disarms that state of awareness.

Continue to radiate and spread Light, for that is what you are!

Ascension Symptoms

As the middle of my chest continues to flutter, like a small bird trying to get out of the cage, I too am striving to break totally free of this dimension. Perhaps you feel the same. Yes, we are moving forward at an alarming rate of progress, toward the Light. Do not feel alone in the journey.

Ascension means a change in perception. Sometimes, during times of increased geomagnetic activity or planetary alignments, ascension symptoms seem to increase. But thankfully, they may not be as bothersome as before. The rate of progress is different for everyone.

This has been an interesting week full of old and new ascension symptoms. Today I woke lying on my stomach, with the left leg raised as if climbing stairs. How delightful to recall that for many years I could only sleep on my back!

My physical symptoms started with a feeling somewhat like the flu. Nearly falling over with exhaustion, there were many times when I just had to sleep. Next, I had face rashes, which I attributed to prescription drugs. There were literally times when I'd wake with multiple red splotches covering my normally pale cheeks. Now, years later and free of the thirteen drug prescriptions that ruled my life, I occasionally see a few red splotches, after a night of restless sleep filled with odd dreams and messages. Today, my body feels lighter, as if gravity is loosening it's effect, while the atoms within my skin jump erratically about like a sailor abandoning ship.

We are moving toward the consciousness of Christ knowing we are connected as unique parts of One. Some of us are fully aware of the process, while others may not recognize the signs. As the DNA in our bodies change so too does our state of awareness. In a nutshell, the DNA in our bodies changes as we more closely align with Source. The change from carbon-based to crystalline allows us to function much more efficiently in higher frequencies.

Ascension Symptoms, Again ;-)

New patterns of sleep permeate days and nights. Tiredness often overwhelms me near eleven o'clock in the evening. Sometimes I fall quickly asleep only to wake every two hours, for the next twelve, to wet my parched throat and use the bathroom. Sometimes, sleep claims me once again several hours after rising wide-awake in the wee hours of the morning. Naps after breakfast or in the afternoon often seem necessary.

It helps to know that ascension symptoms are all about increasing states of awareness and moving on. Today, as usual, I disappeared into another world soon after drifting off to sleep. Quickly moving words rolled past closed eyes as consciousness seemed to bring me back while resting in the Lazy Boy chair. It was a download of some kind. Of this, I am certain. Exhaustion continues. But after nearly an hour's nap, I do not want to succumb to sleep again. At least not until nightfall and it's only 4:30 PM.

Physical symptoms during 2011 brought an increase in face rashes, vision and hearing changes and severe heat in bottoms of feet. Changes of appetite and in sense of smell occurred as well. Emotional, mental, and psychic symptoms varied throughout the year. The need for isolation lessened. The year 2011 also brought an increased awareness of guidance upon waking and sometimes during the wee hours of the morning to 'activate' by bringing more Light into the body. This practice continues for it's vital to reactivate the Light within, which expands through the body and goes out into the world.

Some ascension symptoms in 2012 were odd and yet somehow familiar, severe dry throat, thirst way beyond usual and rising frequently to void more than drank. Waking while breathing oddly and hearing words, seeing symbols or numbers also occurred. Heart irregularities, such as increased erratic beats or sensations, accompanied bouts of increased body warmth. Body temperature wavered greatly from overly heated to frigidly cold.

Erratic habits include a mixture of insomnia, sleeping more than usual, waking frequently, and feeling the need to nap during the day. Thankfully, forgetfulness no longer bothers me nor does disconnecting with family and time. Messages of Oneness, Love and Light are more abundant. Recalled dreams and what seem to be prophetic dreams still occur along with bleed-through to lives lived in other realms of existence. Yes! We continue to transmute and purge all those things not for the higher good, ridding our soul of all karma, never to have to return.

Full moons, equinoxes, planetary alignments and bouts of high geomagnetic activity (including solar flares) usually cause increased symptoms including erratic sleeping patterns. Waking between two and five o'clock in the morning often occurs during onslaughts of increased cosmic energy. Intestinal symptoms vary from indigestion, bloating and gas to stomach pain and nausea upon waking during the night. Sometimes ascension symptoms appear in the guise of excruciating headaches or 'restless body syndrome' a state where it's hard to settle down. Foot reflexology during these times seems to help.

As the body morphs closer to Light, there's often a strong desire to change eating habits. Many people become vegetarians. I eat more fresh organic vegetables and fruit but also consume protein in the form of seafood, eggs, cheese, chicken, turkey, and occasional organic beef or pork.

Continually ask for ease and grace and the process becomes easier in time. Walking and grounding (by sitting barefoot in Nature), gardening and wearing a crystal are two things that help me with the physical signs of ascension. Search the Internet for other methods to deal with these indicators of changing consciousness.

BEing Is Centeredness

"BEing is centeredness."

These words came to me in August of 2008. I had no idea what they meant. A quick Internet search helped me to understand the concept of centeredness.

Centeredness is a state of peaceful awareness allowing us to keep our spiritual core untouched by circumstances. By controlling our energy, we remain in tune with our spiritual nature and no longer project fears or desires into our perception of the world. We also remain unmoved by changed surroundings. Since everything is energy, outer events adjust themselves to our inner control. Stronger centered energy always overshadows dissipated, reactive energy.

Many people reach this state of constant peaceful awareness through meditation, the art of learning to live from one's center. Regular meditation centers and raises consciousness and strengthens the aura. And at some point, I believe, we can live our life in constant meditation, in other words, centered without meditating in the usual ways.

Centeredness is a state of detached BEing, where we see and at times humanly experience things but do not react. For when we react, either negatively or positively, we feed not only the circumstance but also the state of awareness that keeps us in a limited physicality. We may not all wish to end this game of earth life. But centeredness is the desired state for humans seeking to complete the cycle of birth and death.

Several questions may assist to help one decide what to do before reacting to circumstances.

What purpose does this serve?

Is my reaction feeding energy that no longer serves?

Am I ready to let this circumstance go without my feedback?

There will never be a more opportune time to remain centered. It's time to recall and experience the unlimited life of Divine Self. Knowing we are ready to move on can lead us to the perfect state of BEing that once was ours in all aspects. That state of BEing never left. We just forgot that it existed.

Being Present

Living in the present moment is vital because the thoughts we think have the power to create our world. Time and space are illusion. "Now" and "Here" are the only valuable commodities. The present moment is before time was and will be when time is no more.

Like humans, every day is unique and filled with possibility. That makes it even more vital to live each day in the "Now" for it only happens once. Living in the "Now" affords us with a greater desire to make conscious choices, and take responsibility, rather than looking for others to blame.

Being present in the "Now" is a doorway into inter-dimensional consciousness. Some souls, before human birth, choose the experience of living as humans in the "Now" through Alzheimer's or other memory disorders. The present moment offers many valuable qualities such as no history from the past or agenda for the future. Filled with peace, and stillness of heart and mind, we rely on inner strength rather than logic.

Being present in the "Now" is a state of true centeredness, being seen and known for whom we are now, accepting everything as a moment of gratitude. We become more open to the potential for magic and transformations in this state of awareness. Merging with the experience, we reduce energy loss by avoiding emotional tricks and unwanted power games. Living in the "Now" affords the opportunity to connect deeper to our Self, all life forms, and the Creative Energy surrounding us. This enables us to reach our full potential as a multi-dimensional being.

BS

Many of us are being asked to let go of what no longer serves the greater good or our True Self so it's time to take stock of current situations, belief systems (BS) and behavior patterns. Our true essence begins to shine through as we use intuition more, continuing to release anything that does not serve the greater good or us.

Many so-called laws separate and pit humanity against one another. Is the state of separation the way you wish to live? If not, then it's time to change outdated beliefs. We put ourselves under a false premise assuming there are laws other than Gods. As noted by Tara Singh in *Commentaries on A Course In Miracles*, man-made rules may be necessary for society to function but are based on insecurity and fear. Under the Laws of God, he notes, everything extends and creates because everything is One Life extending itself in numerous forms and facets. Nothing is outside of it and everything is in harmony within it.

Most people unwittingly obey tainted BS nurtured throughout the course of humanity's evolution. Many of these outdated beliefs are tools of control to keep us in limitation, willing to give our power away to others who *appear* more able to handle the responsibilities of caring for us. The process of letting go what is no longer relevant or useful includes abandoning outdated BS, destructive habits and behavior patterns. Consider these questions if you're ready to begin the process.

Is there an excess of "baggage" holding me back from accessing my True Self?

Are there habits and items that I just can't seem to do without?

Do I insist on nurturing relationships that no longer serve the greater good or me?

Am I out of the days and nights of drama?

Do I fully trust in my intuition as opposed to looking outside myself for answers?

If you sense the path to self-mastery is yours, begin to move into it more fully by letting go of clutter, habits that no longer serve you, your history, and "baggage." Assess relationships, your atmosphere and beliefs, and change them as necessary. Scrutinize anything that creates an emotional reaction.

There has never been a more opportune time to let go of the old BS harbored for so very long. Changing beliefs and behavior patterns clears the path of energy from dysfunctional emotions and allows us to become a co-creator of reality. These outdated beliefs are ones of restriction and separation, of pain, of unnecessary suffering. We must relinquish these beliefs now before the end of days turns this world into a state of Oneness again. This is a necessary process for all of humanity. We must each take responsibility for our own game of life and realize we hold the power to change it.

Changing Ego's Role

Through eons of time, egos helped humanity to experience and express, and to expand the richness of *All That Is*. But now it's time to end the experiment and return to the Oneness of I AM.

Ego's job is to create an atmosphere of separation that includes rampant negative emotions. Knowing this makes it easy to see how many of us choose to avoid the voice of our soul through the avenue of addiction. We use addictions to mask fears and block emotions. Any addiction deprives others, and us, of true intimacy with *All That Is* and limits the potential for full realization of the soul.

Knowing the potential for addictive behavior helps us to express the True Self within more readily. Some addictions many people do not recognize are constantly talking, exercising excessively, perfectionism and faultfinding, being a martyr, workaholic, or professional patient dependant on others. In my experience, the best way to avoid addictions and address ego is to feel and express emotion, recognize it as part of the human experience, let it go and then focus on positive activities.

It's best not to actively ignore the ego. We must acknowledge that ego helped us to survive in the world. Address the ego by telling it how grateful you are for its help in getting you though rough situations in the past. Since these phases are now complete, tell ego it's time to rest and enjoy the passenger seat while True Self takes on the task of driving your physical vehicle.

When ego is in charge, it's impossible to silence the small mind within. Acknowledging thoughts and replacing them with positive ones works well. Sometimes when ego seems difficult, thank it for the suggestion before moving forward to a constructive endeavor. Allow it little victories like locking the door at night but draw the line at waking thoughts that reek of separation.

Participating in positive, nurturing activities helps us because the more we dwell on ego's negativity, the more we try to kill it, the more we recognize it and make it real. Repeating a positive mantra or affirmation keeps ego busy when the small mind refuses to be still. "I AM grateful. Grateful I AM" is my favorite. Music, writing, reading spiritual books, participating in constructive endeavors like gardening or keeping company with friends of like mind also helps to keep centered in Christ Consciousness.

The trick is to get into the habit of overlooking ego and thereby ignoring it without realizing what you are doing. It's a sort of mind training, the same way our minds were trained to believe all the things we believe now. The same way we trained our mind to forget the True Self when we first came here.

Changing Perceptions

"You can change your perceptions of earth very beyond what you have here."

The message above entered my mind upon waking one morning in 2006.

Opportunities to adjust perceptions and beliefs continue to increase. Yes, we can change the way we think about the world and ourselves! Permanent change comes through altered perception. Our mind is a distribution center for the entire Power-in-Action of the Originating Thought, giving us the ability to manifest at will. Since the characteristic of Spirit-Intelligence is Thought, changing our perception to more closely align with *It* changes the world we experience. New experiences lead to insights that help change perspective creating a different perception of events.

Perceptions are built on the basis of experience but it's impossible to see what we do not believe. We affect our world with thoughts and changing the way we think changes the world around us. By opening our mind to other possibilities, observing our world differently than ever before, we create a new world. Author Neale Donald Walsh notes a change in perspective makes it possible for us to change everything. Perspective creates perception, which forms beliefs. What we believe generates our behavior and subsequently our experience. Experience creates the reality of our life. Remember, as perception and beliefs change, experience creates a better reality when we think positively focusing on the Oneness of all humanity.

Humanity plays a role in the earth's evolution. As Fort Lauderdale, Florida, Reverend Charles Dean Geddes notes:

"Energy fields shift belief systems and you can help to make the shift. There are many mansions in the Infinite Reality that is the Eternal, the defining of God. Everything is perception. As life forms, the Light dispels the darkness. Healed misperceptions dissolve in the Light. Be mindful, Light dispels darkness. Our purpose is to dispel darkness and be free. Ignorance results in pain and suffering from misperceptions. Remember, the Truth, the Light, the Originating Substance."

The new world of greater Light continues to expand but we must open our minds and change our perception to see it. Changing our perception makes it possible to be at peace regardless of circumstances. But we will not perceive the new world with fearful, closed and limited minds.

Ultimately, we are here to recognize that we are a unique part of Spirit, God, whatever name you choose to name the unerring and perfect *All That Is*, in which we live, and move, and have all BEing. As our perception changes, so does our way of experiencing the world so it truly is a matter of changing our awareness to form newer and more positive beliefs. Beliefs are imagination's fuel, for the more we think of them, the more they become a part of us. Once our perception changes and we recognize perfection in ourselves, we are less apt to give our power away to others.

All things are possible with limitless thinking. Universal Energy belongs to and works with everybody. We can master every condition by changing our perception of how we see it because our reactions control what happens in our world. Yes, through the power of thought, we change the circumstances around us. The moment we stop thinking of an issue as difficult it becomes easier to deal with and eventually disappears. Although some issues take longer than others to master, I've found that this is true. We are a part of this indestructible energy that many people call Spirit. Once we realize the divinity within we set that energy free to show us we are unlimited in all that is good.

The more we train our mind, the simpler it is to connect to our True Self but first we must remember that it *can* occur. Tuning in to higher thoughts is much easier when our mind is clear of clutter from negative thoughts, things, and people. My quest towards positive thought started by changing the kind of music I listened to and accelerated as I refused to read the newspaper or watch the usual television. With practice, it becomes effortless to tap into that consciousness in which we live, and move, and have all BEing. It's a learned behavior, like anything else, but this learned behavior is much more rewarding because it frees us from limitation.

Changing The Game Of Life

We are much more powerful than one could ever imagine but have forgotten our true nature as perfect unerring fragments of consciousness. Life on earth is much easier having faith in the oneness of all living things. Once we're fully aware of our unity as one perfect, powerful BEing we no longer require guidance from a source outside ourselves. The knowledge of our oneness as perfect Love, unlimited in power and grace, offers a new perspective that nurtures all life.

Certain segments of society are quickly learning that we hold the power to change the game of life. The only thing 'set in stone' is our return to Oneness and that appears to be happening sooner for some people than others. Changing the rules of the game by rewriting the script creates greater possibilities and brings us closer to the unity we seek. Use these tools against the negativism of duality to help change the game of life.

* Ask to wake up in a reality more spiritually advanced than the one you go to sleep in.

* Thank your True Self for guiding all thoughts, words, and deeds throughout the day upon waking.

* Meditate daily to stay in tune with *All That Is*.

* Maintain positive thoughts to reap positive experiences.

* Employ an attitude of gratefulness and joy.

* Be a channel for Power to work through.

* Learn the joy of infinite supply by freely giving happiness, service, peace, and love.

* Contribute to the positive aspects of this illusion more frequently and use your spiritual gifts for the highest good of humanity.

* Work with others to spread Light and Love throughout the world.

Christmas In Solitude

Servitude and the 'completion track' have drawbacks, which I am now experiencing while in human form. Although I often do not mind, it does seem more difficult to bear seclusion during holidays. And yet, the message is that every day must be, once again, a holiday season, where we treat one another with love and respect.

Long, long, long ago when we first took on these human forms we treated one another much differently than we do today. For one, separation was nonexistent. We felt one another's energy fields so much more easily then and knew of our Oneness. We trusted that everyone in our path held, and acted upon, the Light of *All That Is*. We knew, without a doubt, that we were parts of this great BEing experiencing life in individual, unique forms, and yet, One. Perfection was normal. We celebrated gratitude for life as the gift that it is and all beings knowingly acted as part of the vastness to which we belong.

Many of us now nurture that Light, which we all hold within, and know the times, as Bob Dylan sang, "they are a' changing." Each day brings many more souls to the realization of our Oneness. Each day we live on this planet brings more of the good of *All That Is*. And it is this good that we shall live in for the rest of our journey here on earth.

We each play a role in awaking humanity to the Oneness of BEing. Some souls chose to play the game a bit longer than others did. Some chose to leave suddenly in states of mass confusion while others chose to linger drawing others into their drama. Each soul's role merges with the others to make the blessing of life sweeter. All come to play the game willingly, knowing human birth will erase their memory. And yet, many more humans are now awakening to the nature of true BEing.

Many of us now live within the greatness of having our needs met. They may be simple needs, yet, always met without concern for tomorrow. Many of us know of what's to come. And even knowing face the next so called calamity without fear. We know the Truth of our BEing shines though any storm or ill-advised condition of existence.

The time of Oneness moves closer with each passing moment. And although we may have times of seeming separation, where others experience life much differently than we do, those of us on the 'completion track' know that sooner or later everyone will join the Oneness of *All That Is* once again in all aspects. And so, that makes spending Christmas alone much easier to bear.

The truth of our Oneness is eternal. Today, and every day, know that you are part of something much greater than you could ever imagine. You are never, and have never been, alone. Spirit guides, guardian angels and soul family travel with you wherever you go.

Consciousness Transcends Space

Living as a human is not as straightforward as it seems for upon birth varying degrees of spiritual amnesia force us to forget our true nature. Each finite physical body hosts an eternal soul that bases different lives on what it wants to experience. As unique parts of *All That Is*, souls help one another learn that everyone is innocent because physicality is not our true form. The primary goal is to experience unconditional love through space and time.

Humans take turns living various roles throughout many lives. Our soul plans each life very carefully before coming into human form. Everything evolves around the Divine Laws of Love, Balance, Order, Cause, and Effect. As souls, we choose what family to be born into and when the day and time of birth will be. We create our life by what we choose to believe. And we choose when we will leave our physical body behind. When a soul chooses to transition it leaves despite earth ties.

Consciousness transcends all space and time. Souls agree to play roles because their eternal love is an unbreakable connection that passes through every barrier. Souls agreeing to play 'special love' or 'special hate' relationships help one another to learn the primary lesson of unconditional love. Those appearing to play 'bad guy' roles are spiritual friends and allies. Unconditional love is our true nature. What we think about others as humans is what we believe about our self. Remember, we live in a dream world of our own making so the next time someone irritates you contemplate what you need to change within your own self of one.

Depression Is Old Energy

Many years ago, as I relished in the luxury of depression, it seemed impossible to meet the day with any energy or enthusiasm. Blaming others, always pretending I had no control over what happened, ruled thoughts. Memories of what used to be spurred the depression to spiral out of control. Absolutely nothing seemed worthwhile as I spiraled toward a total loss of direction and purpose.

Ego ruled, for whenever I experienced a lack of love my mood was depressed and anxious, anything but wholly joyous. Thoughts carried me further into a state of despair seemingly controlled by outside forces as everything dear fell away. This experience was not new. But this time, it was very different because absolutely everything changed. Not a morsel of my old life remained to grasp. My old comfortable way of living quickly disappeared while experiencing crises, job losses, financial stresses, and relationship breakups.

Changes really motivated me to improve life. The power within to change every aspect of living then surfaced. I acknowledged it and knew. Finally, it was time to change the way I thought and behaved. It was time to trust in the process of growth, to have faith that I held the key to life within me. I reviewed past experiences, recognized my role in them, and decided the old way of thinking and feeling no longer served anyone. Clearly, the world was changing quickly and past feelings of discord, anxiety, turmoil, depression, and futility no longer suited me. They helped teach lessons but there was no room for them now that they served their purpose.

Focus rested on positive things as I did my best to ignore a fear-based reality. Putting the past aside allowed me to take responsibility for every aspect of life. I cleaned the slate by forgiving everyone who I thought might have harmed me. Eventually, I asked them to forgive me for thinking out of line with the Self within humanity. Life began to improve while living in the moment appreciating what I had.

A variety of things helps to change depression into joy. Potted and flowering plants, pets and positive signs (such as "Life is Good") and life-affirming music always helps. Reading positive books, painting, gardening, building or creating something, singing, dancing, walking or doing other exercise, writing, meditating or sitting still while listening to soft music without words helps lift thoughts as well. It's also very helpful to avoid television and news and to fall asleep to life-affirming music.

The powerful Presence of *All That Is* lies within and taking the time to "tune in" helps to feel it. Realization that I only felt whole when consciously connected with what many people refer to as God or Spirit came soon after forcing myself to walk though the doors of a spiritual living center.

Life here is a game that we agreed to play forgetting the nature of our True Self. But now it's time to remember. We are all the same in *Reality*, parts of each other, parts of one perfect, loving, Whole. Feel into that essence for it is the reality of the One within.

Detach From The Drama

We are in the midst of a spiritual awakening led forward by synchronicity. Our world is a holographic universe that contains all possibilities. Dr. Christine Page author of *Spiritual Alchemy* notes the hologram is a product of light beams that creates the illusion called matter. Our thoughts make this so-called matrix. Nothing is solid. Everything is here but we need to raise our consciousness to find it.

Everything is a different form of the same energy and energy forms around thoughts. Collective awareness produces new holographic images all the time. Since thought creates our reality, it makes sense to pay attention to what we focus on.

Negative thoughts, such as fear and separation, keep us focused on external events. These thoughts are not of the Omnipresent Consciousness. It's vital to remember that, whatever we concentrate on feeds it. We starve the game of separation and mold a better world by avoiding negative energies.

It's much more difficult to hear our Divine Self when the ego keeps us focused on external events. Concentrating on the wholeness of One is easier to do when we replace lower vibrating habits with new life-affirming ones. Replace old habits that no longer serve to make room for higher vibrating energies and detach from the drama today.

Dreams Are Helpful Clues

The True Self waits for recognition. It reaches out in a variety of ways, such as dreams that offer us hints of things to come or a "heads up" in times of turmoil. We all have dreams. But the trick is remembering them so we can glean the messages hidden within those thoughts. Documenting dreams offers physical proof of True Self's guidance.

Dreams are valuable tools if we choose to use them. For instance, many times dreams either gave me extremely valuable advice or offered glimpses into the future. Several dreams told me not only when I would move but that I'd lease a house. They even gave me glimpses of what it looked like. Dreams offer evidence of "bleed through" where my essence wakes me to recall living other lives. They often encouraged me with glimpses of a happier, more abundant future and hinted at what I'd be doing now as we move quickly back to the blissful state of Oneness.

We now receive much more assistance from what many refer to as "the other side of the veil." Sometimes departed family members offer us gifts but we remain unaware of their guidance because we are just too tired to remember our interactions with them. Many dreams of departed family members clued me into the importance of documenting dreams. Yeah, I know this is a temporal mind illusion but as long as we seem to be here, we might as well pay attention to clues that help us to lead a more joyful, loving, healthy and abundant life.

Do yourself a favor and set aside more time to tap into the Source of One. It's always broadcasting. We need only to tune in to hear messages that offer us the freedom we seek. Pay attention to your thoughts, dreams, and especially to the people you interact with while seeming to sleep. Try not to make sense of or judge your dreams just record them for future reading.

Meditate or sleep more. As you meditate, or before you fall asleep, decide what kind of guidance you prefer. Some people ask a specific question while others may want to hear from angels or a certain departed loved one. Asking to hear a message for your highest good is always beneficial.

Evolving Humanity

At some point in time, something within us persistently declares there's more to life than what we detect with the usual senses. A cellular memory of being beyond physical manifestation in the perfection of Oneness lies within. That formless consciousness is part of *All That Is* or whatever you care to name *It*. *It* has no name, no boundaries, and no form. *It* is unerringly perfect and unchangeable.

Humanity entered into separation from *All That Is*, forgetting the essence of our True Self, upon crossing the threshold of physicality. As humans, and as souls, we put too many layers between *All That Is* and ourselves. In Truth, there is no separation and our inner calling is to end this illusion.

Edgar Cayce said, even though we take on various forms in different dimensions, we are "as light, a ray that does not end, lives on and on, until it becomes one in essence with the source of light." Based on the teachings of Michael, we are fragments, individual parts of total consciousness, striving to know more about itself through the game of separation. As fragments, we joined to form entities of about 1,000 fragments who share their consciousness and experiences.

Ego rose from the perceived separation and feeds on our continuing belief in disunity. A great disservice to humanity occurred when ego invented words. They became a way to communicate for the density of form became too much. Words promote separation for they came into being with thought, which came after the perceived separation from *All*

That Is. Thought is the movement of ego, independent of *All That Is*.

The time to recognize that we are spirits in human form, having a physical experience is here. Words are unimportant layers of fake reality but now we can use them to awaken and realize this is an illusion of our own making. Words coupled with our sixth sense leads the way out of the illusion.

Everything is energy. Gregg Braden reports in his bestseller, *The Divine Matrix*, our world may be a projection of events happening in an underlying reality, a reality we change with the energy of thought. Things intuitively sensed and seen related to the future may alter due to positive thoughts and deeds. Thoughts even transform the possibilities of deeper realms into physical reality.

Time is not linear. The basic teachings of Michael note billions of parallel universes, co-existing in the same space, but in different space/time fields than ours. We are living many lives, human and non-human, simultaneously, in other realities parallel to this one. A new parallel universe spins off, assuring each personality that all possibilities play out, every time we make a major decision. Our souls work through these many layers of reality at the same time affecting others lives as well as our own.

Our true nature is Love, pure unadulterated, unconditional Love. But ego gets in the way of recognizing this. Other planes of consciousness love and protect humanity. Acknowledging the awareness of these realities brings us closer to the truth. Ultimately, all is one, all is here, and all is now.

Walter Starcke, author of *It's All God*, reminds us to be grateful for this state of being. "Thank God," he notes, "that this world is a parallel universe to which we can return not only for a refresher course when we need it, but also where we can rejoin our human/spiritual friends for a class reunion and share our experience with those who are still bewildered."

Everything is part of the Greater Plan. The old world is quickly collapsing as more and more people no longer believe in the old story of illusion. Conscious evolution, being aware of our role as co-creators with the process of evolution, is spreading quickly throughout the globe. In her groundbreaking book *Conscious Evolution*, Barbara Marx Hubbard explains a strategy that changed the doomsday approach to one of a positive nurturing shift of consciousness.

Millions of people now realize they have a role to play as nurturing co-creators for a better world. Many groups work all over the world to make this a more nurturing place to exist. World-changing harmonious events are a joy to participate in as people from all over the globe bring forth *All That Is* from within to evolve the world to a state of unconditional love.

Get-togethers create positive, loving, energy filled opportunities to nurture humanity, our atmosphere and beyond. Although each group has their own way of reaching out, their collective power assures our goal of evolving humanity, consciously, and ethically. New proactive groups form periodically but the ones I am most familiar with are Hubbard's Foundation for Conscious Evolution (BarbaraMarxHubbard.com), Redfield's Global Prayer Project (CelestineVision.com), and Joseph Giove's Common Passion (CommonPassion.org).

Good Vibrations

Space Weather News reports (http://spaceweather.com) verify something I have suspected for years. We do feel the effects of solar eruptions. During the early hours of August 1, 2010, NASA's Solar Dynamics Observatory recorded a complex global disturbance on the Earth-facing side of the sun. Most of the sun's northern hemisphere was involved in the event, which included a long-duration C3-class solar flare, a "solar tsunami," and a massive filament eruption. As a result of these blasts, a coronal mass ejection (CME) headed toward Earth. Another solar eruption on August 7 affected Earth as well, as evidenced by data from the Solar and Heliospheric Observatory (SOHO).

Synchronicity prevails and what occurred to me later on a hot August evening verifies that solar events affect us much more, and sooner, than suspected. I've experienced similar things after solar eruptions but never thought to synchronize the solar events with the experience. Before I relate this experience let me just note that I am not a Star Trek fan nor is it my practice to seek help from what some refer to as "aliens."

Sometime during the evening of August 7, 2010 I was awake and aware, lying in bed with closed eyes while being with two Beings. One said something to the other about preparing me to receive more energy, to prepare two points so I could accept more energy. Sensing they were my third eye and crown chakra, I immediately thought, "Well let me position my body first."

I was lying on my back, with a pillow under my thighs, and was going to adjust the pillow to become more comfortable. My arms were at my sides. All of the sudden my body seemed paralyzed. I couldn't move no matter how much I tried. My entire body began to lift off the bed while I thought I was going to fly around the room! It levitated and hovered about two inches off the bed and then shook from head to toes like it was plugged into a light socket. My entire body intensely vibrated for several seconds. At one point, I became aware of a triangle-shaped light in my third eye for a few fleeting seconds before my body stopped vibrating and returned to rest on the bed. The entire event lasted for probably less than a minute.

Throughout the happening, I was enormously thankful knowing that my body was receiving more Light, more of the Light of what we are because we are really, literally, Light. We just came here to play a game and now it's time to return back to Oneness. It's time to return back to Light. This time, we're doing it while still in the human body. And I am so grateful to be one of the illusionary souls that volunteered to show others that it's possible.

Holographic Reality

Science (not to mention intuition) increasingly suggests that we live in a holographic reality. Our thoughts make this reality. **Thoughts go out into the ethers of space to form based on the number of people who believe in them and the strength of the thought.** Humanity is now changing this reality into one based on unity and love rather than fear but it will take some time to fully manifest.

Consider this the next time you focus on something. Consider first, is this a life affirming thought? Do I want this in my world? If not, then thank the thought for coming into your field of reality before telling it it's no longer a part of your world. Next, consider building the world you wish to live in by imagining it first. **The more effort and feeling that you put into this world, the quicker it will manifest.** And remember, do not share what you wish to manifest with anyone not of similar mind.

Let Your Dreams Be Your Guide

Everything we experience is subject to how the brain chooses to process it. Thoughts reflect either the higher vibrating energy of love or the lower vibrating energy of fear. The more we concentrate on any one subject, the more it will show up in our dreams, and subsequently our reality.

Dreams hold the key to freedom but they can also take us into a downward spiral if we focus on fear. They can control us through mass consciousness, or dreams can effortlessly glide us through this matrix, so it's important to pay attention to them. Remember, dreams consist of times spent in parallel dimensions and other realms, messages from the True Self, and what the brain processes of daily activities. Nightmarish dreams are either prompting us to change our thoughts or carrying us through the process of transmuting negativity from other lifetimes. Reviewing and changing daily activities/thoughts can sometimes help to avoid nightmares. Are we spending leisure time in positive ways to nurture our self and humanity? Or, do we pay attention to and broadcast negative activities and thoughts?

For many years, I lived in the darkness of depression, self-loathing, great negativity and futility. Lower vibrating energy ruled my world until I learned there is so much more to experience than we can ever know in human form. I finally stopped concentrating on what seemed to be happening around me and changed my reality and this stopped the nightmares. Yes, new higher energies fill the void whenever we let go of lower vibrating behaviors!

The same energy makes everything. We are ultimate creators manifesting new visions of wholeness but we must pay attention to daily thoughts and activities. Our thoughts create our reality for we sustain energy by concentration. Let me put that in another way. Everything we think about gets our energy! Constantly asking one question can help guide us through this maze of life on earth. "What do I want to feed with my energy?"

Choosing to experience a New World living from the heart rather than sustaining the old reality makes sense. Embracing higher energies of unconditional love, gratefulness, peace, joy and abundance nurtures the True Self. Choosing to be positive focusing on good, Light and Love is a worthy effort.

As noted by Dr. Albert Ellis, "The best years of your life, are the ones in which you decide your problems are your own. You don't blame them on your mother, your environment, the ecology or the President. You realize that you control your own destiny."

You can control your own dreams and destiny in a whole new way once you begin to concentrate only on the positive things in life. Continue to draw in the energy of One for that is what you are.

Life Is But A Dream

This morning's dream further awakened me to the fact that life is a game of illusion. Everything is devised to keep me believing that I'm a human, not a soul having physical experiences to evolve. Some people unknowingly serve to keep the game of separation alive by noting that others suppress us, lie to us, and further strive to keep us "dumbed down." The truth is, there is no body, and there is no soul. And I am beginning to wonder about spirit. The one thing I know for sure is, there is One in which we live, and move, and have all BEing. That One appears as part of *All That Is*, was, or ever shall be.

Earth life is something like a virtual reality game. It all seems so very real but it's not. Everything is just illusion, a figment of imagination. There's much more to life than any of us will ever know in the mind/body state. This physical arena is an exercise in soul growth designed to help us grow spiritually.

However, as long as "we" believe there is a body, "we" can consider the possibility that it is only our brain, the small mind of one, which imprisons the body. Thought is the only thing that stands between the greater good and us. It's time to rid ourselves of the accumulated thought and feeling of the ages operating through us. A change in mental reactions, especially those rooted in feeling, eventually frees the mind to thoughts of greater good.

There's still work to be done before a state of Heaven eternally exists if our life is less than perfect. Thoughts change when we look at things differently. "We" have not "been lied to" or suppressed. Thinking this only serves to keep us imprisoned in a human body where "we" pit "us" against "them." Free will offers us a different way to think.

Taking responsibility for our self makes all the difference. We reap what we sow so it helps to change patterns of thought. Change confused thought patterns with statements of peace. Fearful beliefs change with thoughts of faith while thoughts of happiness and joy thwart unhappy ideas. Loving thoughts always transmute notions of hate and hope banishes doubt.

There are many different ways to perceive circumstances. My grandson is quick to tell me, "Think out of the box Nana." This is the best advice I can offer to anyone seeking a better life. Think out of the box of common beliefs. Find things to be thankful for and blessings in times of perceived loss. Pay attention to messages from other people for they deliver crucial hints about what to remember. Remember, "we" are One. What "we" say or think about others "we" say or think about ourselves. What "we" do to others "we" do only to ourselves.

Lightbody Activation

Clear your mind to experience this light activation fully. As thoughts arise, store them in a wooden ship that sits amid calm seas. Place all concerns and people that come to mind on the ship. Allow the ship to drift away while you take this journey into the sea of consciousness. You may choose to close your eyes and listen to this podcast at: http://www.LightworkersLog.com/videos/LightbodyActivation.wmv.

Feel a sense of lightness fill your body as you drift upon the sea of consciousness as if lying on a float in the ocean. The seas are calm as your body rocks slowly upon the float. The ultimate Heaven, nirvana, lies ahead. There's a knowing that your float knows exactly where to drift as your body feels at peace with the elements of Nature. You soon come to a place of perfect union with nirvana, the supreme experience.

A huge shining circle beckons you forward. There's an arc of golden light that stretches to embrace you as you look into the circle. The circle fills with golden light before your eyes and then expands to cover everything, including you. The all-encompassing light embraces you in a perfect state of Oneness. In this state of BEing, you are aware of pure peace, yet exquisite emotion.

It is impossible to experience thoughts of separation. Nothing exists as a separate piece of matter. Everything joins in perfect continuity within this Perfect Environment. Cozy warmth is all around you. It is of you and through you. There is no up or down as you float in warm soft clouds. Brilliant

Light rays in ever-changing shades and hues flow within the clouds. The pleasure of good fills your senses as each ray bathes you with its light. This nirvana is where you belong for it is Home.

All the colors of the spectrum continue to come and go. Each color brings a different relaxing or restful happiness. Ruby-red rays of light prompt meaningful thoughts of something beyond what you know as light. You move slowly and effortlessly through the cloud listening to Music that surrounds you. The Music is around and within you. And you vibrate in harmony with *It*. You are a part of *It*, and *It* is you.

This purity of Truth is the longing, nostalgia, sense of destiny that you felt when you longed for Home, now fulfilled. You are Home where you belong. Familiar others are joined, bonded to you, with a great single knowledge of Oneness. They are you. You are they. Gentle waves of Love pass effortlessly between you filling you with a completeness of Love. You are Home where you belong in perfect balance.

It is time to activate the Light of Oneness. Brilliant white Light now flows through every part of your being. You sense this Light, moving effortlessly throughout you. The Light is a familiar part of your True BEing and you welcome it with immense joy. It moves in waves, filling you with a sense of completeness, of Oneness with all things. This Light of Wholeness holds the memory of your Lightbody perfection. You may activate this Light at any time you wish for this Light is you. It is the Light you will take back with you to complete your earth journey. Bask in this Light now. Bask in the memory of your Lightbody perfection.

Now it is time to return to your float. The memory of how to activate your being with the Light of Home remains within as you drift upon the calm seas of consciousness. Far off in the distance, you see the wooden ship that houses all thoughts, concerns, and people left behind. Will you allow yourself to chart a new course? Is this the beginning of a new adventure? The choice is, and always remains, yours.

Inspiration derived from *Journeys Out Of The Body* by Robert A. Monroe.

Living In Harmony

We live in a world of duality where everything is energy. Physical bodies are shadows of our divine essence, each on certain vibrations out of tune with higher frequencies, unless we take the time to reconnect with *All That Is* in all aspects. Recognizing mis-perceptions helps us to purge their lower and more densely vibrating energies to raise our frequency.

The Essence lies within always prompting us to see beyond the illusion to recognize that we are gods of matter. Experiencing darkness spurs us forward by offering the contrast needed to search for and create something new. Suffering is an indication that we are out of harmony with our Self, with the Law of BEing. The sole use of suffering is to purify, to burn out all that is useless and impure.

Our natural Self knows the truth. Opinions, judgments, unforgiving thoughts and fear do not exist within *All That Is*. Fear is one of the greatest denials of the Reality of *All That Is* and a barrier to growth. It came into existence when the illusion of separation began. Fear is our identification with the body, values of the brain, and personality. But it's not natural to us.

Fear often transforms a functioning, beautiful physical being into precisely what it fears. It's always the cause of illness and places an incredible burden on the physical body. We begin to experience great moments of illumination when finally ridding ourselves of fear. The body is able to function harmoniously when fear no longer disrupts it. We remember who we really are as the veil of forgetfulness lifts, spirits having a human experience.

Darkness offers us opportunities to transmute lower vibrating energies not in alignment with the purest version of ourselves. Chaos always leads to the creation of a better world. Many people who seemed hopelessly apathetic now search to better their lives because of the darkness souls agreed to create. Darkness is merely a degree of Light unaware of the Love within.

We recognize traits in others that we possess. Everything we hear, even the inner voices speaking to us, comes from our own small selves. The situations we face are the ones we create in our own mind.

Open your mind to a new way of thinking. Learn to clear and clean darkness through forgiveness, allowing your soul to move further along the path of spiritual growth. Harmonize with *All That Is* more fully. Thank people who offer necessary experiences to spur humanity towards the willingness for positive change more in tune with our true being. Allow your heart, your own inner wisdom, your own intuition, to be the final authority and trust that **you are God**.

Musings On Karma

This world is a temporal illusion. Our greater portion exists in the world of Light. Individual souls separated from this unlimited, unified energy, in the process of creating various life forms. Focusing on creations, humans became trapped in the physical and lost their connection with the higher vibration, unlimited Source. This led to concepts of duality and karma, cause and effect, as a means to eliminate the artificial concepts of good and evil.

Ernest Holmes and others note karma is the Law of Cause and Effect, the compassionate dynamic through which we learn to create responsibly. It's neither good nor bad, and when we choose the cause, that choice includes our choice of an effect. Things that the individual sets in motion through the law ultimately "swing back" to the thinker.

Karmic Law works through the Medium of the World-Soul and is the result of how humans use their mentality. This mental tendency is both individual and Universal. Soul contains a record of our inherited tendencies and experiences. Although these memories represent the subjective tendency of life, we can change this predisposition with constant effort and a determined persistency of purpose.

Karma is not a balancing of books but material to transform. It's a mode of learning, the set of circumstances chosen in each life to find areas not yet in Truth. Emmanuel notes, as our awareness deepens, cause and effect come about more rapidly until the process of balancing is instantaneous. At that point, cause and effect cease to exist and there is only

Truth. We are merging back into that glorious state of being now.

Many people seem to be going through circumstances, which seem beyond their control at this time. These things are not beyond their control, for again, everything is truly in our mind. Our world is made of thought and we mold that world with thought. It's important to know that if one is struggling, with situations that seem beyond their control because of others, that they recognize the world is made with their own thought.

We come into this world as souls seeking, most of us, seeking to balance the karma created long ago. And yet, karma is just another thing in the illusion. We need not struggle. We need not continue to stay in a situation that no longer serves us. We need only to be true to our self, that one lovely Self of *All That Is*. It is the only truth that there is. The one Self serves all for we are each a part of the one Self. We all know this one Self. It's just a matter of recognizing and tapping into it.

Karma is a game of balance we choose to play when we come here. And if situations don't improve, despite everything, every effort we have made, we don't need to continue to suffer. We need only to make the best possible effort to keep things positive in our own mind.

And so, if you are one of those struggling in a situation, which seems beyond your control, consider using the power of thought to change your circumstances. Position yourself in a place where you have only positive interactions with others and yourself. You do this by maintaining positive thoughts. Turn off your televisions. Turn off your radios. Stop reading the news. These things only serve to keep you in the negativity of this dream. You can create your own positive dream by focusing only on positive things. I've done it so I know it can be done.

OMG, So Relating Now!

Life changed drastically on April 1, 2012. And now, nearly two months later, the reason finally occurs to me. It's all about facing fears and relating to what seems as pieces outside of me, the rest of humanity, for unless you experience these things, you have no idea what it feels like. That's what this is all about. Well, part of it anyways…

You see, in 2008, I found a way to escape the hectic pace most people seem to live. I dropped out of the usual matrix of living a mundane life, of taxes, banking and receipts, of needing others, of the necessity to leave my sanctuary (except for fresh foods, of course). It didn't come easily but over time through lifestyle changes, positive affirmations and visioning. Right before being booted from my sanctuary with a mere 36-hours to move, by what appeared to be a greedy landlord thinking he'd quickly sell the home I'd so carefully filled with Light and kept up over the past four years, I even found a way to pay utility bills with cash.

I was ecstatic to be on my own, without care or reason to seek outside myself, or physically communicate with others. Yet, my soul (illusion that it is) and it's plan to assist in morphing closer to Truth, knew it was time to move out of my treasured comfort zone right when I'd think there couldn't be a worse time. After all, I was fully prepared to sit in relative safety in the security of a pristine atmosphere, leaving only to stock up on fresh vegetables and fruit, at least through 2012. Ah, but once again my soul knew it was time to move on and evolve.

Looking back now, it's easy to see how synchronicities and listening to intuition made the move so much easier than it could have been. The path since April Fool's Day (yeah, the joke's on physical me) has not been easy. Clean, comfortable places to stay at often seem impossible to get. And the few offers for sanctuary came from people living in limitation I did not care to share. Yet, they too were chances to move forward by recognizing that limitation no longer fit into my lifestyle.

Obviously, not everyone drinks spring water, buys organic food, or possesses a reverse osmosis water filtration system to use for cooking, washing fresh foods and ice. And of course, not everyone concerns themselves with planting fruit trees and organic vegetables.

However, does everyone live in dirty houses with peeling paint, filled with smells, mold, and clutter (sometimes stacks of it throughout the room and even under the bed)? Does everyone need an animal for company? Is it too much to ask for a clean bathtub and private time to use it? Perhaps I'm spoiled but isn't air-conditioning necessary in Florida, particularly in the summer months? And most importantly, are the lightworkers who live as I did too fearful of sharing their space with people of like-mind?

These questions occurred to me with each offer of sanctuary. Yet, each place I ended up at benefited from the Light I spread. Isn't that a part of what this experience is meant to teach, to spread Light regardless of circumstances? Isn't part of this experience meant to help me face unexpected circumstances and still be able to expand instead of contract?

Apparently, despite this physical body's preference, my soul chose to do more than just sit in a safe, clean, pristine ivory tower, write articles and books to raise people's vibrations, do counseling, podcasts and movies, design web pages and upload everything to various websites.

Quite honestly, I do not like the change for numerous reasons. Physical activity increased from twenty to eighty percent during these past two months and I've stayed at more hotels than I can recall. It now costs more than twice as much to live and ten times the number of people cross my path each day. Times spent since finding one of my visioned places in another state have been less than desirable. I now anxiously wait for contractors to build my next pristine sanctuary there (even knowing it may take much longer than expected).

Today's experience, and ego's reason for writing, included necessary visits to two local banks, avoided like the plague for years. Does everyone look the other way when being charged and fingerprinted to cash a check drawn on the bank it came from? Is it just me or does someone else see though the lack of privacy the so-called privacy act claims to peddle? Yes, I see how some people may think it's the only way to live but fortunately others do not and are now striving to change the 'system.' Still, I cannot help but think how everything will soon quickly morph to the Oneness we all use to know so well.

All that's left for me to do is to continue spreading the only message that matters. We are One. There is no other. Those appearing apart are really sections of our selves, waiting to be recognized, accepted and loved. Forgive them if you must but know that they reflect a part of you. And realize those reflections do not, in any time, way or form, need to reflect anything but Truth, wholeness, beauty, joy, peace, prosperity and love.

Roller Coaster Ascension Ride

As I listen to a coffee and questions segment hosted by Steve and Barbara Rother (Lightworker.com), while trying to finally sleep, it occurs to me that many others experience what seems to be never-ending, and in fact ever-increasing, ascension symptoms. Welcome to the erratic, roller coaster ascension ride!

Some ascension symptoms I've lived with for many years while others are very new. Nerve issues, times where it feels like burning (as in hot feet), or pinching about the legs, was new to me during 2011. During 2012, exhaustion filled most days. The year 2013 offers increased intestinal distress but better sleep. Surprisingly, some symptoms remain even after processing and transmuting whatever arises. Many symptoms occur most during times of earth changes, solar flares, or geomagnetic/planetary activity. Sometimes these symptoms appear during a night of restless sleep, waking repeatedly to remember what some people refer to as very, vivid dreams.

It's clear that many dreams consist of times spent on other realms. Yes, many of us work during sleep, connecting other parts of us, communicating messages of Oneness. We are transmuting and clearing many lifetimes all at one time! It's one of the reasons why many more hours than usual are spent in bed.

Keeping odd hours and living on the edge is not a concern when in my own sanctuary. But since April 2012, life has been challenging as I seek out new places to reside. Doing transformational work, and clearing discarnate energies, used to seem natural but now feels unnecessary. Explaining my lifestyle to others, without a clue of what is occurring, is quite another matter!

Physical symptoms vary widely. It makes no difference why they occur. Dealing with them is the issue of late. Generally, symptoms decrease when outside exploring Nature. Other grounding techniques include placing your tongue flat on the roof of your mouth (ever noticed this upon waking?), forming a circle with your forefingers and index fingers, and looking out of your third eye. Always drink plenty of good quality water, eat healthy live foods, go with the flow, and BREATHE.

Physical symptoms listed here are ones this mind/body knows well. Undoubtedly, there are many others including emotional, mental, and psychic signs. The list includes helpful remedies. Some symptoms have been so severe at times that family, if they'd known, would have insisted I visit a medical facility. Since I am pretty much out of the 'sick care system', it is not a preferred course of action for me. Of course, if you feel inclined, seek medical/dental assistance for this advice stems from my own experience.

Symptom	Particulars	Possible Remedy
Aches & Pains	Mainly body joints and spine	Biomat, Epsom Salt Bath, Linden Herbal Tea, Reflexology, Massage
Ascension Diarrhea (watery and explosive)	Usually occurs after transmuting lower energies and shifting into a higher state.	Replace lost fluids & * potassium, Ginger Tea
Ascension Flu (Atypical)	Shifting into a higher state.	Rest & Fluids
Abnormal	Entire body	Hot bath, Biomat, Massage

Body Coolness		
Abnormal Hot Flashes (heat radiates from chest)	Transmutation symptom	Cold washcloth on chest
Breathing Irregularities		Stay calm & BREATHE
Burning on bottom of feet	Grounding symptom	Ice packs on feet
Coughing & Sneezing		Stay calm & BREATHE
Dizziness and loss of balance	Grounding symptom	Eat dark chocolate.Ground in Nature. Grip walls to go outside!
Ear/Hearing Issues	Popping/draining/ringing	Pull lower ear lobe & open and close mouth repeatedly
Electrical-like Vibrations		Stay calm & BREATHE
Frequent Urination	With disturbed sleep	Replace lost fluid and * potassium
Heart Irregularities	Heart-opening symptom	Stay calm & BREATHE
Intestinal Issues	Gas, bloating, discomfort	Ginger Tea, Baking Soda
Insomnia/ Disturbed Sleep	Transmutation symptom	Melatonin or Magnesium (250 mg)
Itchy/Tingling Scalp		This will pass :-)
Middle Back Pain	Heart-opening symptom	Ground in Nature or place a crystal there :-)
Motion Sickness	Multi-dimensionality	250 mg Powered Ginger
Nausea	Heart-opening symptom	250 mg Powered Ginger
Organ Flutters	Organ detox symptom	Stay calm & BREATHE
Profound Exhaustion	Transmutation or shifting into a higher state.	Sleep as needed ;-)
Restless Body Syndrome	Grounding symptom	3/6/9 Omega Capsules (2- 1,000 mg with o.j)
Sensitivity to sounds, smells and tastes	Pituitary/Pineal symptom	Get use to it ;-)
Skin Rashes	Organ detox symptom	This will pass :-)

Teeth/Sinus Issues	Pituitary/Pineal symptom	This too will pass, unless a dental issue ;-) Try AscendedHealth.com for dental issues.
Unusual Headaches	Pituitary/Pineal symptom that rarely occurs but can be very painful.	Feverfew Tea, Massage temples, rest - I admit to taking a pain pill ;-(
Vision Changes	Pituitary/Pineal symptom	Get use to it ;-) Try AscendedHealth.com

* To replace lost potassium, I drink orange juice (o.j.) with added calcium and vitamin D or eat a banana. You can also drink V-8 or tomato juice or eat other high potassium foods such as potatoes.

Note: Ginger tea (made from fresh ginger root) is also useful for nausea and motion sickness. To make the tea, add about a one-inch piece of peeled and sliced ginger to one quart of water and then boil it for 5-15 minutes. Depending upon the strength and type of ginger used, you can use 20-50 drops of tincture to make tea instead. Improve the taste of ginger tea by adding honey and lemon slices.

Signs Of Ascension

Souls choose certain experiences to serve as vehicles that encourage us to let go and reconnect to *All That Is*. The ascension process takes us through many life changes to help our souls evolve. Opportunities to adjust perceptions and beliefs increase and moments of great insecurity occur during times of massive growth in the soul's progression. Changes allow souls to undo past efforts to return to the perfect state we arrived in when first created.

Signs of ascension include disruptions in everyday life including employment and relationship changes, health issues, and location moves. Employment and relationship issues signify changes in body frequencies. As part of the ascension process, some people find themselves in health situations making it impossible to work their usual job. People find it's time to come into balance, take a break, and then find work more suitable to higher ways of being. Working a 'regular job' becomes impossible when it's time to end old roles. Some people get laid off or face other reasons why their usual job no longer matches their body's vibration. Relationships change as well. Soul's purposes and intentions now demand that we pay attention to the plan our soul chose to create, thereby learning that support from others is no longer necessary.

Souls may choose a physical form with a potential for a specific dis-ease (lack of ease) to help with the spiritual growth of self and others. Some live with a condition from birth, while others use it as a release valve, designed to react when life gets to a point where they do not care to go any further. Dis-ease seems to worsen as fears surface along with an increase in body aches and pains. When these signals occur, there's no better time to rectify imperfections and allow the Light within to shine. A health crisis forces us to let go of our usual ego-based ways of control, which opens the way for a greater connection to Source. Health emergencies can impact us, and the people around us, in many ways. They last until we adopt new ways of being, until we align ourselves. Fear and doubt disappear as Divine Love flows through us and we adopt higher ways of being.

Crisis is a learning process in this schoolroom of illusion and the greater the dis-ease the greater amount of love and learning there is to gain from it. The healing of the body in the ascension process requires letting go of all things, even the thoughts we consider our own. Souls may chose dis-ease to offer the opportunity to transcend genetic factors. Our external universe, internal physiology, and perception directly control the activity of our genes. We can control our genes by challenging thought patterns. Bodies are learning devices for minds, changing as we transmute denser energies (fear, dis-ease, limitation, etc.) to allow more room for higher vibrational frequencies.

Non-attachment to this illusion helps us to overcome it. We have the power to transform our environment but need to seek the quietness necessary to go within and restore inner peace and centeredness. Illness often forces us to take the time we need to reject the limited concept, substitute one of wholeness, and realize we are spiritual beings in human form.

Although the body makes its own dis-ease, sometimes illness has a sufficiently strong hold over the mind to render a person temporarily inaccessible to undoing it. Bodywork, using methods such as massage, acupuncture, toning (sound and vibration), and Eye Movement Desensitization and Reprocessing (opening of the crown charka), all work to release physically held fears. The Law of Attraction then works in our favor as we raise our vibration. Lower vibrational energies clear away from us for they are no longer comfortable being around us.

Higher vibrational frequencies continue to pummel the planet with new energies of Light (and these can cause temporary body aches and pains). These frequencies allow us to relate as more open, loving, expressive, and peaceful beings, if we chose to do so. These energies are necessary to transform our physical bodies for evolution. We no longer remain in tune with the ways of old when our bodies become more in tune with these frequencies. The change signifies new ways of being, which result in the remembrance of our soul's planned contribution to humanity and deeper connections to *All That Is*.

Spirit Sense

There comes a time when we sense there's more to life. Many souls design earth life with clues to help them recognize their true nature. Some people may ignore soul's subtle hints while others choose to investigate feelings and experiences. Hints from the Otherside, dis-ease (lack of ease) and relationship issues can be easy to miss. Ever increasing dis-ease and relationship issues occur when we miss those subtle hints to recognize and awaken the God within us.

Health is our natural state of being. However, the soul attracts what it secretly harbors, loves and fears, and body is but servant of the mind. Thoughts make the difference between health and dis-ease. Illness and dis-ease can be a prompt planned by the soul or the result of ego's beliefs and the resulting fears that block emotional flow. Feelings are signals and always have purpose for nothing happens by accident. Feelings can stem from our current life or a previous one. It is up to us to make sense of our feelings, feel them fully and then let them become a welcome part of our total being, while remaining perfect, whole and complete in our mind.

Negativity plays a huge role in dis-ease and anxiety quickly demoralizes the body. The energy required to repress feelings causes a strain in both body and spirit. Resistance creates conflict and causes the energy flow to turn back on itself. There's no conflict if you release your feelings and where there's no resistance there's no harm. We are on our way to improving the world around us when we learn the purpose of feelings that fill us with negativity. Feelings serve their purpose when we let that negativity go.

Ego becomes strong in strife, thrives on conflict, and is happy anytime we react negatively. It's limiting ways stop us from realizing we are from the same source, a part of each other. Fear holds us away from *Reality* as we allow ego's emotions to rule. The original fear we carry deep within is a separation from *All That Is*. Understanding that fears are illusions, and not *Reality*, frees us from the original cause of illness and dis-ease.

We are individualized reflections of Source, a part of *All That Is* and never separate. The time to stop comparing, to stop judging others and ourselves, and to learn the ultimate lesson of love is here. As humans, we recognize traits in others because we share them. These necessary interactions support spiritual growth. We react to things if they bring forth something within us that is a match in vibration. When we hear of somebody dying, or going through hardship, we may feel pain and grief, forgetting our infinite and powerful spiritual nature. Or we may recall our divinity and experience compassion without the pain. The choice is always ours.

Change is inevitable for spiritual growth. There's never been a better time to end the separation game, to be more, to question, grow, and expand recognizing our unity. Claiming our own mis-thought instead of finding fault with someone else serves one best. By paying attention to thoughts, feelings, words, and actions, we conserve the Universal Energy within us making it easy to manifest our perfection. It's merely a matter of changing perception, our awareness of things, to form newer and more positive beliefs.

Replacing negative attitudes with positive ones vastly improves our world for negativity ceases to exist as soon as we stop feeding it our energy. Positive thoughts stop the ego from using us. Cheerful, strong, pure, and happy thoughts build up the body and dissipate ills.

Beliefs are imagination's fuel for the more we think of them the more they become a part of us. Attitudes placing us more in tune with *All That Is* help greatly to experience increasing states of awareness. Ultimately, we are here to recognize that we are unique, unerring and perfect parts of the One in which we live, and move, and have all BEing.

The Art Of Non-Reaction

Today, I'm reminded of the ways ego feeds the illusion of separation. It draws us away from our Divine Self by prompting us to react. Ego then keeps us focused on external events making it much more difficult to hear our Divine Self. Sensationalistic news, designed to distract us, is hard to ignore if we pay attention to media outlets. These reports will cease when the collective consciousness completely transforms to the truth of Unity. In the meantime, it's wise to avoid media outlets and to concentrate on the wholeness of One.

Energy forms around whatever you hold in your vision so the power to transform all lies within you. It's vital to remember that whatever we concentrate on feeds it. Thoughts are power, and we give that power away, whenever we allow the thoughts of others to change our perception of reality. Every time we seek to rectify something, seeming to be outside our Divine Self, we are really acknowledging separation.

Universal Truth surrounds us. We are literally energy, experiencing life in a dense, physical form. We are One. There is no separation and our ultimate responsibility is to nurture earth, and all upon it.

Whenever we let go of lower vibrating habits and behaviors that no longer serve us we leave a space for new, higher, energies to fill the void. Maintaining a certain distance from everyday events helps us to achieve peace of mind. We starve the game of separation by remaining in engaged detachment. To do this, hold a neutral association to any events, while filling everything, and everyone, with pure, beautiful, radiating, white Light. Remain neutral, focusing on the Unity within to re-harmonize.

Nothing is more powerful than the master within. We reconnect with Divine Self by attuning to the neutral pattern of Unity within us. This personal Power cannot be controlled externally. Trust the honesty of the Divine Self. Align with *It*, while Unity removes everything else from your path. And continue to draw in the energy of One for that is what you are.

The Awakening Process

Upon experiencing many life and body changes several years ago, I surfed the Internet to find "Twelve Signs of Spiritual Awakening" by Geoffrey Hoppe and Tobias. It then seemed that life reflected every sign of awakening to a greater state of awareness. Withdrawing from family and friends seemed easy for I no longer fit in the same unhealthy mold. The feeling of loneliness, even when in the company of others, accompanied an ever-present, deep, longing for Home. It was challenging, for I found it difficult to get anything done. Unusual sleep patterns continue even now as physical disorientation and 'self talk' increases.

I've now come to realize ascension is only a change in thinking, which makes it possible to adapt to a higher way of BEing. All the sudden life changes reflected a changing consciousness. This change in perception helped me to view the world differently. I then began to experience the world in more life-affirming ways. After opening fully to the reality of our true BEing, I began to experience peace regardless of circumstances.

In my experience, the process of realizing who we really are starts with the need for change because life is no longer comfortable. There's a strong desire to improve living conditions. Assessment of lifestyle comes next. This results in changing bad habits to more life-giving modes of living. This may mean changing nutritional habits; omitting harmful practices such as substance abuse, smoking, or drinking; reading self-help materials instead of newspapers or magazines; avoiding negative people; listening to positive, nurturing music; or watching inspiring movies instead of watching television.

We create a better life by opening the mind to greater possibilities and thinking out-of-the-box. Learning to control emotions, thoughts, words, and deeds consciously puts us closer to freedom. The next step is to dispel illusions that no longer serve us, such as ill health, limitation, etc. It's vital to take responsibility for what happens in our life, instead of blaming others, and to stop trying to control other people.

The reality of our true nature as spiritual beings, having a human experience, often takes time to recognize. We achieve greater things by focusing on positivity and gratefulness. Focusing on spiritual growth through journaling; affirmations; meditation; prayer; gratefulness; spiritual classes; volunteer work; and blessing others helps a great deal.

The Lightworker's Log Website (LightworkersLog.com) offers a wealth of life-affirming resources. You'll find "Twelve Signs of Spiritual Awakening," and many other resources, at the Crimson Circle Website (CrimsonCircle.com).

The Great Shift

We are in the process of a great shift moving quickly toward Christ consciousness. The earth is moving to a higher vibrational state as it rids itself of humanity's negativity, through natural disasters such as earthquakes, volcanoes, hurricanes, floods and fires. Catastrophic events pave the way for higher vibrating energies within individuals as well. We are here to help with the shift by recognizing and clearing negative energy. We all have different paths and must trust that Universal Law prevails and all things lead back to the Source of utter perfection and reunion.

Time is accelerating in this illusionary world as old structures fall quickly away. We each have a specific role to play in the New World. We are ultimate creators raising the vibration of the planet and manifesting new visions of wholeness. Using our freedom of choice, we decide what to experience and how to react to what occurs. Choices include the higher vibrating energy of love or the lower vibrating energy of fear.

Time we know is an illusion and space as well. Living in a place of consciousness where the illusion of linear time exists promotes the feeling of separation to avoid self-improvement. The shift to heaven on earth increases as we forget patterns of exclusion and move forward in time to its end. The only reality is our Oneness.

Carefully chosen thoughts are the thoughts to nurture. It all comes together when we understand how things work in the collective consciousness. Veils between dimensions are extremely thin and those of the spirit world, who love and support us, meet us in dreams and meditations. Listen closely, for they offer encouragement and guidance at this crucial evolutionary moment. The power of Creation to transform lies within you. Continue to draw in the energy of One for that is what you are.

The Illusion Of Life

We are One living in a state of grace through the power of *All That Is*. The form that represents us is just one of many forms our soul takes on to help us realize *we are not really a form at all*. We are as formless as *All That Is*. We take on these bodies and use them as tools so that we may experience more. So that we may experience what it's like to be in a body.

The illusionary human form allows us a plethora of opportunities to expand awareness. There are so many things to experience from being in a body and this is the only way we can experience them. Yet, in choosing human form we've come to the point where we forget who we really are – an extension of *All That Is* projected into physical reality to experience that which we are not. As souls having a spiritual experience we play the game of human life to create in physicality. Yet, we are unlimited. We just forgot. Amnesia helps us to be less homesick for our heavenly existence and allows us to start each life with a clean slate.

Souls create each life based on the level of consciousness held before birth on earth. Soul agreements before birth determine the souls that will serve as family, friends, and other key people, all based on what our soul chooses to learn. Some souls agree to play easy roles, while others choose challenging roles, which many humans may find distasteful. Yet, we all play different roles to help one another in various lifetimes. There are no coincidences for we plan both major and minor things to experience in favor of soul growth. Reincarnation is the process that allows each soul to experience every human condition as the path to full spirituality and eventually back to *All That Is*. Some souls chose to return to that treasured state sooner than others do.

Although each life offers opportunity for soul growth, the goal, the end of the game, is the same. We are here to help one another experience unconditional love in a new way realizing there is no limitation whatsoever. We are here to recognize our unlimited potential of good as parts of *All That Is*. Eventually, we learn to express our true nature through unconditional love, health and well-being, abundance, joy and creativity.

This is an auspicious time in history as we transcend the limitation of life on earth. Go smoothly with the flow, letting go of all that is not in harmony with Light, as we glide quickly to that of which we truly are. In *Reality*, there is no I, no you, no me. There is no we, no us, no them. There is only One, brilliant, luminous, perfect whole of *All That Is*.

Thoughts Create

Humanity exists within an ever-changing matrix of possibilities. Everything, seen and unseen, connects to everything else and thought contributes greatly to physical experience. There are no idle thoughts. Even the slightest vibration of thought produces form at some level of experience within time and space.

We are creators of circumstances since thoughts draw to us what we dwell on. What happens in life depends greatly on how powerful we know our thought to be and how we portray that thought. Thinking of anyone in a negative way is harmful for thoughts permeate the mental medium between us. What we think about others is really what we believe about our self and what we do to others we do to ourselves so it's vital to train our mind and consider only positive thoughts.

Problems show up as the body's ego attempt to separate, to react and feel things such as guilt and anger. Once we give validity to ego's world we reinforce it, which allows it to thrive. Projection of guilt onto other people is a way of escaping from unconscious guilt. The guilt we feel is really about our seeming separation from *All That Is*, the One in which we live, and move, and have all BEing.

All living things exist within *All That Is*. As a drop of ocean water is part of the ocean, so too are we part of *It*. There is no separation from the One. *A Course in Miracles* explains:

"Your other life has continued without interruption, and has been and always will be totally unaffected by your attempts to dissociate it."

If you know your thoughts are powerful and speak them with great intensity they manifest much more quickly. The "Third Insight" revealed by James Redfield (celestinevision.com) speaks of this dynamic energy noting that thoughts influence other energy systems and increase the pace of coincidences in our lives.

Remember, humanity's true nature is unconditional love. We are here on earth to experience, express, expand, and recognize that true nature. It's vital to thank and subsequently invalidate the ego when problems surface. When we negatively react to what happens we can thank ego for getting us through life and then recognize our Oneness. We can then forgive our self for believing the contents of the ego mind. Sometimes it helps to start by forgiving whoever you think offended you for not knowing we are unique parts of *All That Is* experiencing life in physical form. Eventually we learn; it is only our self that needs forgiving.

Truth As I Know It

Life seems often to be a dream and yet everything here on earth feels so real. Of course, I know it is not. Everything is just a figment of my imagination. Many years passed me by while I thought about how this earth and its inhabitants came to be. I think I have things figured out now, finally after eons of time, I do remember.

The truth is we are lost in a sea of forgetfulness playing a game called earth life. It is not, nor has it ever been, our intent to stay but just to experience, express and expand back to *All That Is*. Sometime back, I'm not sure when, we decided to change the game. Allow me to start from what I now perceive as the beginning.

In the beginning, there was the Word, yeah the Word, the Word of One. But putting that aside, there was a black void of emptiness and fullness, everywhere, including everything. That pure consciousness was all and still is *All That Is*. It somehow began to expand by thinking, manifesting if you will, parts of *Itself* that wished to create more and more richness of BEing.

Those parts decided to separate, in mind, from the greater void. We are those parts, figments if you will, that decided to take on various forms to experience, express, and expand the richness of *All That Is*. This description will spark a light of remembrance within you that will glimmer brightly by the time you finish reading it.

We lost our way. After eons of forms and experiences, after eons of words and deeds, we forgot the nature of our true Self. There is only One. And right now in bodily form, we are a part of One but that One is a part of something much, much greater, *All That Is*.

As near as I can determine, we placed layer upon layer to mask our true Self. It started long before Atlantis or Lemuria. Those were just epic turning points in an illusory history; times when we decided to take on increasingly denser form. Those days are long gone. In Truth, they never existed for this is a game of mind, the small mind in each figment.

As part of this experiment, we belong to a vast entity, Soul. Many call this the Oversoul or World-Soul. It consists of unique and vastly different souls, all playing the game of life on earth. Throughout time, each soul takes on new personalities, new experiences, new missions to experience, expand, and express the richness of *All That Is*.

As souls, we agree to forget our true nature before we take on a new bodily form. Our form and the environment we choose offer us the perfect place to experience, express, and expand. This is just one part of our journey. And now, it is ending. I don't mean that in a negative way but only as a change, as in the change of earth seasons.

We are finally beginning to remember who we really are. Many of us chose to lead or be an example for others to follow. These are monumental times as we awaken to recognize our full potential. Yes, we are indeed Gods of Creation.

Unique Parts Of One

Humanity is one of an infinite number of entities and things that makes the whole of Omnipresent Consciousness (*All That Is*). We live, move, and have all being within this Universal God Soup. There is nothing, absolutely nothing, outside of this soup. But, over eons of time, humanity designed multiple layers of separation. In *Reality*, there are no layers, no outside or inside; nothing that reeks of duality exists. We remain unique parts of *All That Is*, just as a drop of water that flows to the beach is still a part of the vast ocean.

As humans, we agreed to experience this realm of consciousness but lost sight of God-given abilities. In the course of experiencing the dream, we continued to spiral into denser and denser realms leaving the True Self behind.

It's now time to remember who we are and return to *All That Is* in all aspects. It gets confusing because free unique will reigns on earth making it appear that we're separate. More people each day realize this is not the case. However, as we do seem to be in physicality it's necessary to play the game of life. And since we think differently, there's always another opinion, another experience, another way to live.

If one is open-minded to believe beyond a rigid set of beliefs, one will clearly see there is so much more to life than anyone could ever comprehend. Thoughts and words make our physical reality and now that physical reality is manifesting quicker than ever before. That makes it vitally important to remain positive in thought for what we concentrate on manifests to become our reality.

We are reborn, Emmanuel tells us, whenever we allow a new concept to enter our awareness for everything shifts, and rearranges itself, to allow for infusion of the new. Just one new thought or experience makes us different than the moment before. The game changes when we view ourselves as beautiful light beings, pure energy in material form, having a physical experience.

Certain numbers help people shift their awareness. The numbers three and four are prompts to wake-up. Three or more of the same number enhances the energies of whatever level we're on at the time we see them. Among other things, the number three represents the Holy Trinity, the number of the Holy Spirit associated to the triangle, and a favorable number associated with birth (RidingTheBeast.com). The number four refers to creation. It represents the union of the Trinity into One and symbolizes the family, considered as another image of the number one. Symbolically, the square or the cross represents four. It's the symbol of totality and considered by the initiates as the root of all things. You'll see a lot of fours if you don't pay attention to the threes you see. The number 444 holds great symbolism for it represents the first divine woman. It's the call to awaken to our true being. The Resurrection number is 444 or 4444.

It is my understanding that some souls chose to stay a bit longer in the dream of forgetfulness. But it's important to note that *All That Is* has never and will never be disrupted.

One can see *All That Is* as a vast collage of everything that exists. One may take a photo of the collage and make a puzzle but it does not change the collage. One may separate the photo into unique puzzle parts but that has no affect on the collage. One may even disconnect the parts of the puzzle and separate them to the four corners of the earth, and beyond, but it still has no affect on the original collage. Eventually, the puzzle parts will come together and disintegrate having never been 'real' at all. The photo will be no more, but the collage remains perfect, whole, and unaffected.

Humanity is part of the dream puzzle associated with the photo of the collage. Yet, in Truth, we are part of that perfect, whole, and unaffected collage of *All That Is*. Human thoughts are the only things that separate us. Focus on *All That Is*, or whatever you refer to as God, and life here will unfold in perfect, joyful Divine Order.

Weaving Dreams

This illusion affords us the state of sleep where the opportunity to communicate with our soul and connect more strongly with Spirit exists. Based on my experience, dreams consist of times spent in parallel dimensions and other realms, messages from the True Self, and what the brain processes of daily activities. This is important to consider for everything we experience is subject to how the brain chooses to process it. Brain processing includes everything we see with our eyes, hear with our ears, read and react to, and sometimes try to ignore. These things often turn up during the delta state of sleep while dreaming. Strong emotional reactions are more likely to crop up in some form during sleep.

"Dreams must be heeded and accepted," Paracelsus noted long ago, "for a great many of them come true." When we see what could be future events in dreams we can change them by choosing differently. By making that change we wake to a different reality.

For instance, my daughter Rebecca often had a vivid nightmare where my husband James and I drowned after crashing through a bridge in the Florida Keys during a rainstorm. She finally repeated her dream in vivid detail. I slipped it into the back of my mind but brought it forth when circumstances matched her vision. As James and I drove through a sudden rainstorm in the Florida Keys, I had him slow down before we crossed a bridge. No one can say with certainty that we avoided an accident but Rebecca never had the dream again.

Eleanor Roosevelt announced, "The future belongs to those who believe in the beauty of their dreams." But what if our dreams are not to our liking? Based on my experience, we can change the past and future, thereby ensuring a better Now. We do this by revisiting past events to change their memory and by periodically asking to wake up in a dimension with a better outcome for all concerned.

The key to waking up from this illusion is mind training. It's vital to fill your brain with pleasant thoughts before bedtime to weave better dreams. Wide varieties of tools are available to help retrain the mind. Audio programs designed for people to hear at bedtime are particularly useful to break old habits that no longer serve the new reality. Listening to inspiring music or positive affirmations at bedtime helps as well. Waking to recall empowering words with beautiful music is much more appealing than rehashing world events!

What If Life Is An Illusion?

What if life on earth is an illusion of various states of awareness? What if our emotions contribute to the length of our stay? What would happen if we stopped playing the game? What would happen if we stopped being emotional? What would happen if we stopped being so 'mental' thinking we had to figure things out? What would happen if we decided to just BE?

What does it mean to just BE? It means to just live in the Now moment. It means to stop trying to figure things out. It means to stop thinking about changing lives that never were. It means to stop visiting the astral world, the other worlds in which we think we live.

BEing is a state of awareness. BEing, just BEing, is a state of One. It is living in the Now. It is enjoying the moment. It is forgetting there ever was a past, nor will there ever be a future. BEing is Now. BEing is our natural state.

What if the natural state of BEing is to experience, to express, and to expand through loving acts of kindness? One does not need to study. One needs only to BE, to express the God within. Experience, expression, expansion, that is why you are here. You're here to experience and express *Source*. And through that experience and expression, *Source* expands. There is no right or wrong here. There is only expansion and expression through the experience of the soul. Yes, soul is an illusion as well, a required illusion for the body to experience, express and expand. We are One living in a state of grace forever. That is the truth of the matter.

It is always advantageous for the soul to grow, to experience new things. Don't worry so much about being stuck in the dream. Just BE. Just BE without limitation. Just experience new things without remorse. Just live the love you were born to give. **Expansion is in the experience of BEing.**

൫ ൬

CHANNELED MESSAGES

Awesome Power

There are no messages that you do not already know. They are all held inside you waiting to be explored, waiting to be recognized as the Truth that they are. All is One. All is here. All is Now, not left behind or looked forward to, but Now. The energy that flows through you is of the One of *All That Is* that no-named BEing which permeates your entire being and that of all living things.

The Truth is known to all but recognized by few, as yet, comparatively speaking. It is an awesome power to behold within your Self, the Self of One. All are a part of this unending One of which all things derive. Your true power comes from within and that is the message of Now. It is the only message recognized by those that speak the truth of One. Hear ye, hear ye all. The message of One is clear. Speak thy truth from within yourself, the Self of One.

Choose Your Thoughts Carefully

The thought of writing an article on the process of understanding our true essence came this morning. The words below entered my head as I began to write. They came almost too quickly for me to write them down. It did not take long to realize that the process of automatic writing was in process. The exact words heard inside my head are formatted here in a way that makes sense to this physical form.

"There are so many things I can feed with my energy, so many things I could tell you, but I now choose my vocalizations carefully. I know now that everything I think or talk about feeds it energy.

"We are in a time of great change and you can be a part of this change. Consider your actions and words. Consider if you want to continue living the life you live. It is a choice regardless of what you believe. It is a choice to live in poverty. It is a choice to live in pain. You must reconsider these choices and think again. Is this what you want for your life? Do you really want to suffer now that you know it is unnecessary?

"The vast choices before you are beautifully perfect in all things. You can live the life you wish for now the world is your oyster. Choose your thoughts carefully for soon what you wish for will manifest much quicker than ever before. We are in the end of the old ways, the end of humanity's sleep. Listen. Take the time to listen to the Voice within you for it is ever speaking. Know that this is the true Voice of humanity for God is truly all there is. Go forth and spread the word of *One*."

Enriching The Whole

Messages continue and the ones I hear now relate to the concept of transmuting darkness. It is my understanding that we are now in training, learning how to merge with *All That Is*. We are learning how to merge into nothingness, and yet to merge into the unseen everything all around us.

"We heat up our control dramas to the point where we roll off the Whole. The Whole is ever so happy to oblige us as we descend into darkness, for eventually we return more Light back to the Whole having transmuted that darkness. So naturally, it is our honor to come here to bring back more to the Whole. So you see why more are descending to earth at this time. All is in Divine Order. All is well.

"You tend to appreciate the dark side so you can transmute the light. And yet, it is all the same. It is all one Light, one Truth, one Life. The darkness serves in a way unknown to man. The darkness serves as a harbinger of Light. It brings you all to a point of return. And that return is sweet within your soul, the soul of One.

"Remember, everything is magnetics. Just flow with the magnetic force around you. Flow into it. Picture those tiny, tiny, white Beings of Consciousness and merge with the magnetics around you. Merge with the One and know that all is well.

"Your Self came to earth to express its human self, to expand, to express, to grow. Your Self came here to earth to learn, to merge as One is what your Self is learning now.

Consider the possibilities of your highest good. Flow with those that expand your BEing to its highest potential. Expand into the Being of Light that you are. Expand into the nothingness of which you came, turning the darkness to Light forevermore. This expansion is a new game and all are welcome to join."

Lightworkers Unite

The following message came to me on Monday, February 7, 2011. It prompted a thought about physically uniting Lightworkers who finally stopped seeking something outside their Self.

"Please be aware that the earth is changing rapidly and the body within changes as well. Know that all is well within the soul of One for that never changes. Peace is always with you, above and below, within and without.

"You are the thought that builds the world, the image that radiates the Light. Be careful with those thoughts and words. It is time to get together. Focus as One more clearly. It is time to come together and shine your Light. The brilliance of that Light is everlasting. It shines across the land, purifying and cleansing all. Just as you trust in the future of humanity as One, you must trust in the Power within. Know that Power is within you and bear the Light, wherever you go, consciously spreading it across the land. Know the land is your sacred home."

The One

The world is changing at an alarming rate. High solar activity resulted in a series of coronal mass ejections affecting earth during February 2011. A new sunspot emerged quickly to become wider than the planet Jupiter unleashing the strongest solar flares since December 2006. NASA's Solar Dynamics Observatory recorded intense flashes of extreme ultraviolet radiation while brief radio blackouts occurred. Major solar flares continue to erupt on the sun and as they do, the messages I hear increase. These all seem to fit together.

"It is a matter of resonating with the One. You either resonate with the One now, or resonate with the One later. There is no if. It is a matter of resonating with the one Light of all BEing."

"We seek to return to the Light, and yet, there is no returning for the Light resides inside each and every one of us. That Light is everlasting, and if we choose, we can tap into that Light, very easily, and very efficiently. Knowing that all come together as Light in the end of what you call your world, there is no end and no beginning. There is only one pure and brilliant Light to resonate with, to be, to shine. Resonate with the one Light knowing as you do you resonate with the One of *All*."

"There is no above. There is no below. There is only here and now and One, no two. There is no me. There is no you. But you know that in the deep recesses of the mind. The One is part of *All That Is* and *All That Is* is part of something much greater than the One, unimaginably greater, unheard of on other levels. All beings know this."

"This is one final moment coming up before us in the history of humanity, the humanity that never was and never shall be. This final moment beckons the call to those who worship the earth. Heed the call and know the earth is transforming in all its glory. *All* is heard across the land, and nary always, shall heed *It's* whisper of love. Fortuitous events rule the day and night as all transcend this earth of limitation.

"Knowing the One is many, we heed the call to beckon forth a new age within this world of seeming woe. For naught the release of new energies but the changing of the guard occurs. The guard of One controls the beings upon the earth of One. And in this change is made the sureness of humanity's whole. There appears to be no other way to beckon forth this call on an earth filled with beings who sleep within the dream. The dream must end as all good dreams for never was it to be. And though you sit and hear our voice know that she never was and never shall be again.

"The sureness of the return to One is finally here. Heeding wholly, the call to One appears. There is nothing unusual within. But without the call appears startling to those upon the earth of One that never was and never shall be. And now the wholeness of earth is revealed in all its glory, the wholeness of One. The earth is made new again and with this change the end of time creeps closer than ever before.

"A remembering for the One comes through quickly to the whole for the one that is, and was, and always shall be. A remembering of the One is all that is known in eternity. This remembering comes quickly for all and all the truth of their being. Hold tight. Hold fast. The world is changing quickly. And you as well, as a body, change along with this earth."

Welcoming The Energy Of One

There seems to be a dramatic increase in Florida storms. I've learned to welcome them for the rain keeps a lid on the heat and offers energies that spur us forward. Encouraging messages always break through the veil of illusion when these storms occur. Several days ago, I heard:

"It is time to concentrate on the big picture of *Reality*. All things fall away in the true scheme of things. The meaning on this road never ends because it is an illusionary road we call life. The road is in our mind. You're going to go the distance this time. You're home free. In these trying times, the key is faith. Faith is the key to all things."

Lightning flashed in the distance last night as the all too familiar wave of exhaustion overwhelmed me. Sleep soon offered a refuge from the muscle aches and tiredness but I woke within the hour with an ache in my temporal lobe. Once again, my throat felt like sandpaper until I drank from the water bottle on my nightstand. I made my way to the bathroom by gripping the walls to steady myself. This type of activity has become normal for me upon waking during the night for I'm still wobbling between dimensions.

After waking several times over the course of a few hours, it was clear that other energies were refining the new human template. A message broke through lightning and rain:

"It is time dear One. It is time to merge, to merge back with the One in which you live. In the Whole, you are free to grow, to expand, to enrich all around you. Merge with the One. Know you are Light. Know you are the Wind. Merge with the One knowing all is well. Merge with the Good. Merge with the Love. Merge with the Light knowing all is well."

The usual heat saturated my body. I lay spread-eagle upon the bed, anchoring myself with one hand facing up and the other palm down, as my heart pounded in tune to the slight throb in my head. It seemed easy to merge as a sense of lightness filled me from head to toe. I merged with the surrounding air for several minutes before drifting back to sleep.

The sun seems to have disappeared from the sky. Storms continue to surround the area in which I reside. It's raining again. Thunder echoes all around. Yet, I know that the paradise where we live as One remains secure. That place becomes closer to our reality each day. Expand your energy field and merge with the One to feel it.

ଔ ଓ

BOOK EXCERPTS

A Lightworker's Experience

Book Three: Lightworker's Log :-) Transformation

Green orbs drift by during meditation. I'm lost in 'the gap' with no memory of what's occurred until a picture of a box floats before still closed eyes. People are inside the box. They slowly float into a large, blue orb.

I remain in trance for several minutes receiving (what, I don't know), until unconsciously drawing a deep breath. It's as if something unseen directs my physical form, and now, returns control back to me. Familiar upper body heat overwhelms so I kick the sheet off my body to cool down.

*The puzzle pieces of this amazing life assemble much more rapidly two years later. So much has happened since beginning this strange process. I had no idea it was preparing me for what I'm doing today. I am one of many souls who chose to return to this illusion to wake everyone up to the fact that **this is an illusion of our souls making**.*

Blue orbs represent new life. Seeing figures of people restricted in a box (representing the limited earth) float into a blue orb signifies a new consciousness. The vision was meant to remind me of my soul's contract. It activated the process that led me to where I am now. This notion fits perfectly with everything Lightworker sources such as Karen Bishop and Patricia Diane Cota-Robles teach.

Although the global economy seems worse every day, I know it's an illusion we came to experience as souls. The wonderful part is that we **can** *change it with our thoughts. There are thousands, if not millions of people, now praying and treating for a New Earth where money is obsolete and the world is ruled by Divine Love, peace, and harmony.*

I sense the number of Lightworkers is now much larger than ever before and grows quickly with each passing second. Gregg Braden and David Wilcox verify many things I've intuitively known with evidence of scientific research showing how the world around us, and our very bodies, are evolving. I'm grateful to play my role.

Belief Systems

Book One :-) Death Of The Sun

Humans hold certain subconscious beliefs before birth. These opinions include beliefs from past lives. Conscious opinions (ones we are aware of) are based on many things. The environment we're born into plays a role in our belief system. We choose the type of environment we will live in before birth based on how we need to grow as souls. It's up to us to be aware of our ability to evolve once we're in human form. Our environment includes what we learn from caregivers and role models, especially from birth to six-years-old. Peer groups and other people we're with can affect our beliefs as well.

Dr. Christine Page notes people can help us grow spiritually or harm us by taking our sense of self and power away to feed themselves. Beliefs can sometimes be smothered by persistent and aggressive lost souls in current lives. These souls disregard the truth others speak because they feel inferior. They are not aware of the true nature of humans.

Humanity's goals are to love and cherish all living beings, be in harmony with one another, and live in peace without the aggressive, fearful, and destructive threat of war. Our species depends on how well we care for one another. We can help each other by realizing the true nature of our being. We are all Good, we are all Light, and most importantly, we are all Divine Love, a part of our Creator.

Opinions can change based on how we spend our time. What we choose to do and where we choose to go affects our beliefs greatly. Our awareness of what is 'out there' can greatly change our belief system. Fearful people tend to limit themselves by always making excuses as to why they can't do something or go somewhere new.

Keeping an open mind and considering new information helps us to grow. Although it's hard to go out of one's comfort zone it helps immensely to open the mind to greater possibilities. Attending classes or reading 'new age' materials opens the mind much more than reading romance novels or watching television. Sadly, some people may not have the access to new things as easily as others do.

Many people believe that we travel in spirit/soul groups throughout eternity. There's always a spirit from our group nearby when we are in need of direction or protection.

Born To Forget

Book One :-) Death Of The Sun

We are born into human form after choosing the details of our new mind-body life on earth. The tricky part of the process is that we agree to forget who we really are, spirits in human form in a dream. We agree to forget that being human is just a game.

Nothing in this or any universe is what it appears to be. Everything is just a projection of the mind. A 'sick thought system' shared by everyone in this false universe dominates the unconscious mind. Humans are unconscious of the true *Reality*, as they appear to live in a world of duality. Consciousness is the domain of ego.

God didn't create this world of duality, humans did. God knows only unconditional Love so it's not the nature of God to create anything of this world. Humans agree to not wake-up until it is time to do so. We may or may not have fulfilled our so-called contracts when we begin to wake-up. And we may not wake-up until we leave our mind-body. As part of soul's game, if you don't learn your lessons then you won't wake-up to *Reality*, which is natural and abstract.

There are so many clues for us to tap into when we're ready to. Movies such as *Chances Are* and *The Matrix*, songs such as "Serenade" by the Steve Miller Band, "The Wall" by Kansas, and "Silent Lucidity" by Queensrÿche. There are numerous books, commercials and even common sayings with the word 'wake-up' that tell us things like, "Wake-up and smell the coffee." All of these are meant to prompt our little mind to wake-up to the fact that we are spirits in human form, part of One Mind.

Some humans, maybe all humans, choose their own clues before birth to prompt them so they'll 'wake-up' from this dream we call life. I chose to wake-up upon my son's transition. As souls before birth, we made a deal that I would bring him into the dream and he would wake me up upon leaving his physical body. Now, it's my charge to help others wake-up.

So what did you choose to wake you up?

Do you remember?

Breaking Through The Veil

Book One :-) Death Of The Sun

Every chance she got Samantha watched the video she'd made of Daniel. She repeatedly watched the part when they were on a Keys family vacation one night. Being the jokester that he was, Daniel had bought a huge, blackish brown, plastic, palmetto bug. He planned to trick everyone with it.

Daniel attached the plastic bug to the door leading out to the view of the Bay in the morning. It was hard to miss seeing the bug since everyone went out that door. Some of them were frightened but they all had a good laugh. The fake palmetto bug remained a source of laughter throughout the day.

Samantha cried bitter tears thinking of how they would have to bear their first family vacation without him. After a while, she got up to get a drink to get her through the night. She saw a palmetto bug as soon as she turned on the light in the kitchen. It was just about the size of the one in the video and ran across her right foot. She screamed in terror.

James jumped up out of bed and ran into the kitchen. He chased the bug around the room and squashed it with his left foot. It was the first of many palmetto bugs Samantha saw in the house over the next year. They appeared every time she watched the video segment of Daniel's plastic palmetto bug. She finally stopped watching the video but occasionally saw a bold one in her kitchen or living room.

Sometime later in her spiritual progress, Samantha learned that Daniel had been trying to break through the veil to communicate with her. She was so wrapped up in the grief of thinking he was gone that it was harder for his spirit to break through from the Otherside.

Many times the bugs would appear when James was not home. Samantha eventually learned to chase them herself. She killed them and flushed them all down the toilet at first. But then she began to think she was to let them live. They were messengers sent by the spirit of her son to let her know he was still around. She was to treat them with love.

Samantha started to silently talk to them in her mind and thank them for coming. Then she'd let them know they belonged outside and she was going to release them. She told them she would not hurt them. All they needed to do was be still as she picked them up and carried them outside. She used a paper towel to pick them up and as she did, she was amazed that they let her. James really wondered about her sanity when he saw her do it.

Depressed after midnight one night, she opened the kitchen cupboard to get a cup for ice cream. A palmetto bug quickly jumped onto her chest. She panicked immediately, screamed, and brushed it off onto the floor. James was fishing in the Everglades so she was alone in the house. She began angrily cussing at Daniel out loud.

"This isn't funny," she said stamping her feet up and down on the linoleum floor.

"Oh, come on Mom," she heard Daniel reply. "Lighten up. You have to admit it is."

Samantha could see him laughing in her mind. He thought it was funny because he'd scared her more than he had when they were in the Keys. It was his way of letting her know he was still around. She wasn't happy about the way he did it and asked him to find other ways to alert her of his presence. Daniel told her to stop grieving. He wanted her to be happy. He wanted her to have some fun for a change. She agreed to try and then made a new rule that she only wanted to see certain creatures. Her preferred list started out as only butterflies, birds, and cats but soon expanded.

Captured Stuff Of Matter

Book Three: Lightworker's Log :-) Transformation

Results from many scientific experiments show that intentions affect results. Different intentions produce different effects even when everything else in experiments remains unchanged. Unexpected results occur when we don't focus on the process or the results. Intuition can lead us to the same conclusion with physical results to prove it. Allow me to explain.

Unerring guidance over the past few years taught me to listen always to that inner voice. And surprisingly, intuition recently led me to a wonderful discovery. One can record Stuff of Matter, the essence of all things, on videotape.

A few years ago, intuition led me to videotape my twelve family photo albums. I thought it was because a Florida storm would soon destroy them so I laboriously videotaped them over several months. Initially, I taped with the video camera light turned on. Sometimes I used a white or yellow light in the living room. As time went on, I stopped using lights and taped in my sunny bedroom, the room consciously filled (using Spiritual Mind Treatments) with all the Love and All the Good There Is. I still feel the Love surrounding me when I videoed those photos.

At the time it didn't occur to me that I was ridding myself of the past the only way I knew how, to dwell on it and bring up the pain, the hopelessness, and the fleeting moments of fun and love, without commiseration. While taping photos I played music or noted the Presence and our Oneness with *It*.

Photo albums were wrapped carefully in large Ziploc bags before storing them in a large plastic bin after taping. The contents of videotapes went onto a laptop computer using a software program. And then the mpeg files went onto DVDs and I thought that was the end of the project.

Weeks later, something prompted me to use the DVD's and computer files for another project named "Nana's Legacy." Intuition guided me to concentrate on certain pictures putting them into another computer software program. The pictures seemed to change as the movie played but I didn't pay attention to that in the beginning.

Only now do I realize the video captured Stuff of Matter as it swirled throughout my room, while I continually blessed the room and everything, in and around it, with Light, Love, and Good. The undifferentiated Stuff of Matter then began to change within the room as evidenced by colors that affected the white photo album pages and white frames of the photos during the process of videoing. This became increasingly apparent in many of the photo stills lifted from the videos.

By the time I worked on the sixth video during filming, I realized that colors within a single picture changed. Intuition guided me soon after this realization to take certain segments of taped photos and break them down into several frames. Each frame was different, particularly when videotaped in what I now refer to as my "white light room." The changing field within each still photo became clearly visible. Varied hues of blue, reddish-pink, and fleeting yellow continued to amaze me for certain photos are black and white.

Some frames were much different from the ones before showing a color change in the white background of the photo paper. Tinges of blue and magenta appeared in photos along with what looked like tiny faces. The colors deepened over time. Orbs that changed with each frame around people's faces appeared in photos as well.

Spirit also guided me to show the movement of power to illustrate how something invisible is all around us. Certain pictures revealed the movement of power with the display of a blue stream of light moving from one person to another. (Love is the color of magenta, kind of a pinkish-reddish color. Blue is the color of new life.)

Mist appeared in photos as well. There were parts that I played back during the movie, to get pictures and take frames for Nana's Legacy, where there was static, no music, or talking. Those were the times that really showed the mist and the flow of blue or the flow of magenta, sometimes gold. I'm not sure but the gold may have come from the yellow light used in the beginning of the series.

Capturing the Stuff of Matter without realizing it is a wonderful thing to do. I was just trying to extract one single picture off of an mpeg file or DVD video. And yet, when I videotaped the pictures previously these things were in the room and showed up on the video. That's why intuition led me to tape the photo albums.

Nana's Legacy isn't about my path after all. It's about everyone's birthright. We hold the power to change everything around us and there's no better time to use that power. Thoughts and spoken words do indeed manifest into differentiated Stuff of Matter. Positive thinking does make an awesome difference so focus only on the good of *All That Is*.

Comfort And Encouragement

Book Three: Lightworker's Log :-) Transformation

Constantly malfunctioning electronics are often a clue that the energy around us is trying to communicate. An excerpt from *Transformation* shows us one of the ways this occurs.

~~~~

As I work on the book listening to uplifting music, the CD player stops between songs.

"Don't be sad Mom," I hear in my head.

I hold back tears while silently replying. "I am acting sad aren't I?"

I've been home for almost three hours after spending less than that with family at Ruth's. Now, the fireworks are starting. Although I enjoyed seeing Ruth, Rebecca, Samuel, and his buddy, Momma, Terry, Rachel, and Abigail it seemed like I was alone.

"Remember, this is just an illusion, a dream world Mom. You can make it what you want to. You can choose to be happy or you can choose to be sad," Daniel's essence notes.

"I know but it just seems so real," I answer while knowing what I'm hearing is true. "I choose to be happy and enjoy my time here."

As the sun continues to set, I watch a funny movie on the back porch using my laptop and headphones. The movie quickly transports my mind. It's nearly midnight when I shower before bedtime.

Sleep is difficult. I find myself on the Internet at one o'clock in the morning. Two of my friends have sent messages of love. Charles sends a message in bold type font twenty times its normal size. "THE MOST GIANT QUANTUM HUG YOU CAN POSSIBLY IMAGINE!!!!" Sara from Michigan sends a series of funny cartoons that make me laugh out loud before finally feeling the tiredness of the day.

I wake after 9:00 AM unable to sleep more and lie there thinking about my day. I'll write more, that's a given, but what else can I fill my seemingly lonely day with. There's one more plant to repot and I begin to think of a planter from decades ago with a kitten face on it. I rise and find it in the china hutch that Daniel made me years ago. Due to many circumstances it's a miracle to still have it.

The ceramic piece looks much too fragile and precious to use as a planter. My eyes are drawn to a present from Daniel received in the 1990's as I put it back on the top shelf. The sunshine pillow is still in its box sitting next to the ceramic angel that says "Hope." Abigail gave me the angel last Christmas. I pick the box up and lift the pillow out stroking the "You Are My Sunshine" lettering amid the puffy cloud and smiling sun.

A thought flashes through my mind that there's a message for me somewhere that I've never seen before. Reaching to the bottom of the box, I find a slip of paper from a fortune cookie with a quote from Eleanor Roosevelt.

"The future belongs to those who believe in the beauty of their dreams."

It occurs to me that Spirit's clues are subtle but now I'm paying attention.

Placing the paper back, I squeeze the pillow thinking of Daniel and notice the tag that's still attached. "It's just a manufacture tag with information," I think, even as I'm drawn to open the flap. Daniel's beautiful penmanship proves me wrong.

"I still remember when I was a child you used to sing me this song."

My heart melts reading the message. I finally allow myself to cry, once again, for the son I know I never really had.

"I can cry now, can't I?" I ask the air around me. "It's been a long time."

For a few moments, I cry like a mother who lost her child, even knowing his essence led me to find the treasure at this time to boost my faith in the mission our souls agreed to.

"Mom, you're never really alone," Daniel's voice rings in my ear. "You know that we are always with you and you know this is a dream world."

"I want to come Home," I silently repeat while walking over to the kitchen window even as I smile thinking Daniel is already there.

"A few more years Mom."

"That's right. I have to wake up as many parts of me that I can. We are all parts of God and no one can truly go Home to stay without the others. I know I will continue to receive the love and support that I need to finish my work and I'm grateful."

"Go outside in the sun even if you don't leave the porch Mom. Go outside."

Wiping tears from my face, I walk back to the room where the china hutch stands and put the pillow back in its box before opening the sliding glass door. The sweet song of birds at the bird feeder surrounds me. My mood begins to change as I stand in the sun. I know Spirit guides me. Comfort and encouragement will continue to come when I mistakenly think I need them.

Experiencing The Connection To *All That Is*

Book Three: Lightworker's Log :-) Transformation

Many lightworkers feel the familiar connection to Source at sporadic times such as when gateways open. The day after November 11, 2009 was such a time for me. Physical discomfort from excruciating pain in an abscessed tooth made it necessary to take prescribed antibiotics and painkillers for days prior to November 11. This experience appeared to be a purging of the denser, darker energies within.

Since I live mainly in the Now moment, it did not occur to me that November 11 was an auspicious day upon attending a short reading of Rumi's work before engaging in a fifteen-minute meditation. The small group gathered everyone seen and unseen into the room to share and spread Light throughout the world. I called forth everyone I knew, including the members of the Global Prayer Project (meditated with the previous night via Webcast).

The power filling me was undeniable, as I remained grateful for air-conditioning, which offered a steady stream of cold air despite the cooler Florida night. This time when my body filled with heat, it was much more bearable as I held the Light spreading it as the night before.

An hour later, I was home and soon in bed, sporadically rising every fifty or ninety minutes, each time recalling a glimmer of something, but unable to recall what it was. Exhausted at dawn, I rose again and this time remembered.

A voice just told me I was getting more power. As I lie still to receive it, I felt the familiar heat spreading from my heart's center throughout the body. The heat became almost unbearable. This time I did not throw off the bedcovers, but remained motionless, reminding myself of doing this so many times in 2006 and 2007. My entire body was then vibrating as if plugged into a light socket. I have felt this energy before but not, to my recollection, to this extent. And when I thought I could not stand it any longer, it seemed to be over.

I opened my eyes and raised my head slowly still feeling a counterclockwise rotation of energy circulating directly above my head. Again, it's now a familiar feeling, but not to this extent. This strong beam of energy came undoubtedly from Source, the Universal Cosmic Energy that will help to bring me Home again.

Gratefulness overwhelmed me as I thanked God for the experience and for carrying me through it. My brain began to kick into gear but could not deny what occurred. Failing miserably, it tried to convince me the communication was not from Source. But I now know how Source works. It never demands but guides by communicating certain things. It is always my choice to follow up on the communication or not.

Of course, one must be discerning when it comes to hearing messages. Certain things often occur simultaneously upon hearing messages of Truth. One senses a certain vibration around them along with a change in temperature. Messages of Truth such as, *Forget your humanness. Be one with **All**,* come in different forms, but always empower.

For instance, before going to bed one night I posed a question. The 74-degree room felt uncomfortably cold even after putting on pajamas and a pair of socks before crawling under the bedcovers. The answer to my question came when I woke the next morning along with the all too familiar heat that seemed to consume me.

A few days ago, I heard there was an energy field above my head that I could tap into at any time. I need only to remember it. An unconscious deep intake of breath brought me back to full consciousness as my body shook with vibration. It vibrated vigorously for several minutes afterward.

Experiencing White Lightening

Book Three: Lightworker's Log :-) Transformation

"Can you tell me," I ask looking up at Reverend Charles, "what the flashes of light are that I see? They're like tiny twinkle lights."

"Oh, my dear child," he replies softly placing his hand on my shoulder. "You are blessed with the sight of God."

He seems to understand as I tell him about what appears to be tiny atoms circulating throughout the air. When I admit to being *A Course In Miracles* student, he reassures me that the jagged flashes of light are normal for Course students. His hug leaves me wanting more. I rush home to read page 25 of the Workbook for Students in *A Course In Miracles*, which notes:

"My thoughts are images that I have made. You will begin to understand (this idea to the process of image making) when you have seen little edges of light around the same familiar objects which you see now. As we go along, you may have many 'light episodes'. They may take many different forms, some of them quite unexpected. Do not be afraid of them. They are signs that you are opening your eyes at last. They will not persist, because they merely symbolize true perception, and they are not related to knowledge. These exercises will prepare the way to it."

Edgar Cayce, I now recall, once noted in a reading, experiencing "white lightening" the true Light, is symbolic of the awakening that is coming. "More and more as the white light comes to thee, more and more will there be the awakening." The colors seen hold different meanings. White is symbolic of "the light of the throne of mercy itself" while green represents healing, blue trust, and purple strength. Cayce further notes, "Ye may never see these save ye have withheld judgment or shown mercy."

Power Games

Book One :-) Death Of The Sun and
Book Two :-) A Change In Perception

We are consciousness in human form. As humans, we live in an illusory dream world where 'power games' are played. Controlling other people with words or actions often is accomplished on an unconscious level. Usually, people have no idea that they're involved in 'power games.' They just know that saying and doing certain things to other people makes them feel stronger. Energy thieves either forgot how to create their own energy, or lost their spiritual connection to Consciousness, God, the Source, whatever term you relate to best.

Energy theft can lessen a person's confidence, for humans are often fearful when threatened verbally or physically. They feel forced to pay attention to the person threatening them. This gives the 'thief' their energy and helps them to feel stronger, while the 'victim' feels weaker.

Dr. Christine Page tells us, human energy stealing happens all the time. It's "more successful when an individual is shamed, fearful or in despair, for then they will easily surrender their energy to the lowest bidder."

Socially isolated people with low self-esteem and feelings of inadequacy often play the energy stealing game. Bullying is common in homes where those bullied regain their self-esteem by shaming others less able to answer back, such as children, partners, and animals. This type of control over others is damaging and "sucks the vital energy out of those who are being dominated."

People at the highest risk of energy field theft include those with a need to be liked or needed. They may desire harmony at any cost and have a passion to help or change others. Some people may need approval or acknowledgment. Of special note now being much more related to current earth time, fearful people are at high risk of being the victims of 'power games.'

People use four main ways to steal energy known as interrogation, intimidation, sympathy, and aloofness. The method we use to compete for attention in childhood expands into the way we steal other people's energy. Learning our own control drama frees us to become conscious of our actions. We are here as humans to further spiritual growth and can focus more clearly on our spiritual mission upon learning of our own drama.

Humanity is raising consciousness to new levels of compassion and tolerance. It's time to end old world 'power games' and to clear patterns of suppression. We must recall that all negative behavior is really just a call for love. When someone acts negatively, they offer you the opportunity to bless and love them.

Consciously aware humans obtain their energy without stealing it from others. They get their energy from Source and look beyond the control drama to see the real person (spirit), and then radiate loving energy their way. Energy thieves feel that loving energy and give up their way of manipulating for it.

Solar Activity Affects Humanity

Book Three: Lightworker's Log :-) Transformation

Solar activity increased considerably over the years. Researchers link geomagnetic activity to a mixture of strange phenomenon impacting earth and humanity. Common space weather disturbances include solar coronal mass ejection (CME's – clouds of magnetized gas propelling solar material out into interplanetary space), coronal holes, and solar flares.

The geomagnetic field is increasingly unsettled with active conditions each time CME activity occurs. CME's and intense solar flares can cause radiation poisoning in mammals. Shock waves from these events typically strike earth's magnetic field within twenty-four to thirty-six hours.

Anomalies in the earth's overall energetics and magnetism grids will continue to affect humanities electrical energy and electronics over the next few years. Currently in 2010, we are increasingly feeling the effects of solar active regions, experiencing unsettled levels in the geomagnetic field due to recurrent coronal holes. Solar active regions are growing in both white light area coverage and sunspot count.

Research shows solar activity affects humanity. We are magnetic beings and feel electric currents because they change our magnetism. Sensitive humans recognize magnetic fluxuations within earth's magnetic field both emotionally and physically. **Geomagnetic activity disrupts electrical power, causes auroras, affects sleep patterns,**

thoughts, dreams, cardiovascular health, and increases paranormal experiences.

As earth's magnetics change, so do our bodies. Previously, changes in geomagnetic activity wiped out the species on earth but this time the earth will not end. Changes occurring now help Mother Earth to transform into the New Earth. The earth's decreasing gravitational field is also a contributing factor to human enlightenment. **We are evolving energetically, becoming more Christ conscious, knowing we have the ability to move between worlds.**

Only crystalline substances can exist on higher dimensional levels. Karen Bishop notes in *The Ascension Primer* that solar flares bring in very strong blasts of higher crystalline energy – the new structure for our bodies. Crystal makes it possible to resonate to a higher level of divine consciousness. This fiber creates a new internal foundation and is necessary to help us adapt to the New Earth.

Surges of crystalline energy are the most forceful, dramatic, and powerful forms of energy shifts, creating the most immediate change within us, pushing the older and denser energies out. **These phenomenonal energy surges can cause symptoms such as insomnia, anxiety, heart palpitations, severe bloating, and indigestion.**

We now use satellites to lessen the effects of earths constantly changing magnetic fields. Yet, smart power grids, GPS navigation, air travel, financial services, and emergency radio communications can all be knocked out by intense solar activity. Find more information on geomagnetic activity at http://spaceweather.com.

Soup Of God

Book Three: Lightworker's Log :-) Transformation

The World Healing Meditation (repeated by fifty million people first in 1986) escapes my lips at sunrise. The meditation is part of a daily ritual performed after something wakes me to begin the day. I now repeat three powerful words, "Peace, Love, Harmony" sitting in a lotus position on my futon bed facing east, with palms up on crossed knees. Sometimes it's less than a minute before I feel and see the unseen. My palms vibrate as I watch the Stuff of the Universe, the matter of which all things are made.

The day's reading and treating begins by opening *The Science of Mind* to a random page. A yellow highlighter notes the words, before structured prayers (treatments) set in motion the fundamental Law of the Universe, the Law of Love. Decades of formal prayer to a God outside me are gone. I know treatment expands consciousness, clarifies, and lets in the realization of Spirit. We connect to this Vital Life Force through treatment, and soon realize we're one with *It*. Using the Law of Love, I now consciously plant seeds in the subconscious Mind, knowing with God all things are possible.

Just repeating the word God makes a positive difference. In one of his groundbreaking books, *Life and Teaching of the Masters of the Far East*, Volume 6, Baird T. Spalding notes:

"Light and life is all one. You must give it one name always. You can never think of these things but that your body is vibrating at a higher attitude."

A sense of separation from God keeps us here, so we need to look beyond the body to correct our disbelief in Oneness. God's energy is everywhere. Every time someone says "God" the body's vibration changes. And although the word for God is spelled differently in other countries, the letters have the same vibratory influence. When we pray in full dominion, not begging or demanding, our body falls into line and we become the God within. The most definite statement we can use is, "I Am God" or simply "I AM."

Suggestions For The 21ˢᵗ Century

Book Three: Lightworker's Log :-) Transformation

* Make personal responsibility a necessity in your life; start by caring for yourself and your birth family.

* Always put love of people, starting with yourself, before love of material possessions.

* Recognize that you have the power and knowledge within you to make your life better. Stop pride from limiting personal or spiritual growth.

* Always ask questions no matter how stupid you, or others, think they may be.

* Practice Mindfulness:

Value love, peace, and harmony among all living things every day.

Think about the consequences to others and yourself before you speak; choose words carefully.

Think about the consequences to yourself and the world before you act; know that your actions can affect people you do not even know.

* Always love all living beings without remorse; act through love and not anger. Give more than you take; lend a hand to lift other people up.

* Help as many people as you can throughout your life to nourish the spirit in all people.

* In times of need, first help people who wish to help themselves; help all people if time and finances permit you to do so. Do not enable destructive people to hurt themselves and others by helping them repeatedly as they continue to destroy themselves and others.

* In times of loss or trouble always look for the lesson that can be learned.

* Be prepared to see opportunities for personal growth; take them and put your fear aside. Opportunities for growth that create the most fear are the ones that offer the most positive growth. They always nourish your spirit the most.

* Assure that the world is a better place before you pass on.

* Remember, there are always spirit guides to help you choose the most positive ways to help yourself and others. To tap into this knowledge, focus on your heart with good intentions for all living beings. Offer love, peace and harmony to everyone you meet.

The Power Of Thought

Book Two :-) A Change In Perception

We possess the power to create joy amidst confusion, happiness in the mire of disappointment, and peace in a world of war. Van Praagh, in his book *Reaching to Heaven* notes, when we declare ourselves victims living in fear, anger and resentment, we attract situations that create more of the same taking us further away from God.

Knowing that telepathy stretched much further than the communication shared with my children changed how I thought in later years. Thoughts increase by giving them away and the more people who believe in them the stronger they become. We send out thought-vibrations all the time. Those thoughts go out into the ether to affect others. As like attracts like in the Thought World, we reap the results of thoughts and attract things, circumstances, and people who think like us. Once we realize the Law of Attraction, the power of thought, we can rest safely and calmly unaffected by the turmoil around us.

A Course In Miracles teaches that we can't possibly be a victim of this world because we invented it ourselves. We view the world as we wish to see it so all we need do is change the way we see the world. I refused to take responsibility and stop blaming others, but remained full of resentment, remembering the past and unable to enjoy the experience before me. Life would have been much easier if I'd known that it was all a game we chose to play before taking on physical forms and that by changing my perception the 'victim mentality' segment would end. Viewing situations in a different way made it possible to improve my world significantly.

Your Choice: Project Or Extend

Book Two :-) A Change In Perception

A Course In Miracles reminds us, as humans we either project or extend. Feeling distanced from everyone, ego made sure to project my issues onto someone else. Projection, to the ego, is a means of getting rid of something it does not want. In truth, it's the fundamental law of sharing by which we give what we value in order to keep it in our mind. The ego always tries to preserve conflict by projecting it from our mind to other minds. However, we cannot project conflict because it cannot be shared. Giving it away only insures that we keep it. The belief that by seeing it outside of us we exclude it from within us is a complete distortion of the power of extension.

Anger and attack come from an attempt to project responsibility for our own errors. Projection means anger, anger fosters assault, and assault promotes fear. That is why those who project are vigilant for their own safety. They are afraid that their projections will return and hurt them. Believing they have blotted their projections from their own minds, they also believe their projections are trying to creep back in. Since the projections have not left their minds, they are forced to engage in constant activity in order to recognize this.

The land of separation beckoned once again. Instead of seeing how chaotic this first Christmas season was for Rachel, without her husband, I thought only of the limitation my family seemed to experience. Jealously and anger took the place of compassion and love, as ego automatically switched again to 'victim mentality.'

What we see in others is a reflection of our own consciousness. Projection is a way we use to cast our fears and lay our shortcomings onto others. The more we project how we feel about ourselves onto others the longer it takes to help our soul advance. It was not clear to me at the time how the refuge of projection placed me in a prison apart from everyone else. I now see the pain others were dealing with that I in my own pain failed to see.

The thought that we all choose our lives here is comforting. **Judging any experience as unfair always leads to separation from others.** At this time, my mind refused to recognize the abundance of opportunities to change the world around me. 'Victim mentality' stopped me from creating happy experiences to fill life with gratitude and joy. It never entered my mind that experience would change when my responses to what happened changed.

CB BO

REFERENCES

Atwater, P.M.H. *Beyond the Indigo Children*. Vermont: Bear & Company, 2005.

Bishop Karen. *The Ascension Primer*. 2006.

Campbell, Dan. *Edgar Cayce on The Power of Color, Stones, and Crystals*. New York: Warner Books, 1989.

Cayce, Edgar. "The Readings Say: Color and Healing." Venture Inward, July/Aug 2009, Vol. 25, No. 4: 44.

"Coaching, the Art of Being Centered," October 31, 2006, (organisationandspirituality.wordpress.com).

Cornell, Bharat. "Meditation: The Art of Being Centered," (ananda.org).

Foundation for Inner Peace, *A Course In Miracles*. California: Foundation for Inner Peace, 1992. (ACIM.org).

Page, Christine. *Spiritual Alchemy*. London: Rider, 2003.

Rodegast, Pat and Judith Stanton. *Emmanuel's Book II The Choice for Love*. New York: Bantam Books, 1989.

SAM. *Book of One :-) Volume 1*. South Carolina: CreateSpace, 2013.

SAM. *Lightworker's Log Transformation*. Indiana: Balboa Press, 2010.

SAM. *The End of My Soap Opera Life :-) Book One: Death of the Sun*. South Carolina: CreateSpace, 2013.

SAM. *The End of My Soap Opera Life :-) A Change in Perception*. New Mexico: Eagle Spirit Publishing, 2009.

Starcke, Walter. *It's All God*. Texas: Guadalupe Press, 1998.

Zukav, Gary. *The Seat of the Soul*. Audio tapes, 1990. Audio Renaissance Tapes, Inc. Distributed by St. Martin's Press, New York.

ABOUT THE AUTHOR

SAM, intuitive author of the "Lightworker's Log Book Series," is a minister (ordained by Sanctuary of the Beloved Church Priesthood and Order of Melchizedek), channel of higher realms, teacher, founder of SAM I AM Productions (SamIAMproductions.com – – assisting humanity to find the Divine Spark within), and administrator of the popular Internet resource Lightworker's Log (LightworkersLog.com). Spreading Spirit's message of Oneness throughout the globe, SAM is a wayshower helping others to learn the truth of BEing so humanity can return unique figments back to *All That Is*.

The Lightworker's Log Book Series

Book One: Death Of The Sun

Book Two: A Change In Perception

Lightworker's Log :-) Transformation

Manifesting: Lightworker's Log

Prayer Treatments: Lightworker's Log

Adventures In Greece And Turkey

Earth Angels

Return To Light: John Of God Helps

Bits Of Wisdom